Think Again

Also available from Continuum

The If Machine, Peter Worley

Philosophy for Children through the Secondary Curriculum,
   edited by Lizzy Lewis and Nick Chandley

Philosophy in Schools, Carrie Winstanley and Michael Hand

Philosophy with Teenagers, Patricia Hannam and Eugenio Echeverria

Teaching Thinking (3rd edition), Robert Fisher

Think Again

A Philosophical
Approach to Teaching

John L. Taylor

Foreword by A. C. Grayling

continuum

Continuum International Publishing Group
The Tower Building 80 Maiden Lane
11 York Road   Suite 704
London SE1 7NX New York NY 10038

www.continuumbooks.com

© John L. Taylor 2012
Illustrations © John Horner, 2012

British Library Cataloguing-in-Publication Data
A catalogue record for this book is available from the British Library.

ISBN: HB: 978-1-4411-2106-6
   PB: 978-1-4411-8775-8

Library of Congress Cataloging-in-Publication Data
Taylor, John L. (John Lees), 1970-
Think again : a philosophical approach to teaching / John L. Taylor ;
foreword by A. C. Grayling; cartoons by Jon Horner.
  p. cm.
Includes bibliographical references and index.
ISBN 978-1-4411-8775-8 – ISBN 978-1-4411-2106-6 –
ISBN 978-1-4411-5132-2 – ISBN 978-1-4411-6262-5 –
ISBN 978-1-4411-3488-2 1. Philosophy–Study and teaching. I. Title.
B52.T29 2012
107.1–dc23

                 2011040413

Typeset by Newgen Imaging Systems Pvt Ltd, Chennai, India
Printed and bound in India

To Georgina

Contents

List of Illustrations

Figures

Tables

Philosophical entry points

Subject Area	Page References
Art and design	13, 108, 116
Biology	89, 104
Business studies	12, 114
Citizenship	44
Computing	108
Economics	114
English	11, 107, 110
Extended Project	15, 89, 91
French	12
Geography	60, 107
Health care	74
History	59, 109, 110
Languages	108, 110
Mathematics	108
Media studies	108
Philosophy	23, 29, 36, 91
Physics	12, 29, 102, 107
Psychology	13, 108, 112
Religious education	91, 100, 108, 115
Science	108, 112
Sports studies	40, 77

Foreword

In a world of startlingly rapid change, flooded by vast quantities of information and misinformation, with new demands and challenges pouring over us more quickly than we can anticipate, we are certain of only one thing about the future: that we know very little about what we will be asked to do, know and contend with as its changes speed towards us. Most people studying now will be repeatedly asked to learn entirely new things during their lives, and at least as often they will change careers as a result: and the things they will have to learn, and the jobs they will do, have not even been invented yet.

In light of this, the overwhelming need in education today is to equip people with the ability to learn and relearn constantly, to be flexible, adaptable, good at identifying the nub of challenges and problems, good at working things out, good at asking sharp questions and good at knowing how to find answers. In short, they will have to be good at – *thinking*. The overwhelming need in education today is to equip people with a genuine ability to think.

This is not a mere cliché. Bertrand Russell once quipped, 'Most people would rather die than think, and most people do', but as with most of his quips it is stingingly accurate. In fact, rather than helping people to become real thinkers, today's education seems to place obstacles in the way of their becoming so, by submitting them at both school and university to an endless round of compartmentalized preparations for exams, so that instead of education they get training – training for jumping through hoops with the chief aim of getting into the best version of the next stage of the same thing.

And in the process a large point is being missed. The great ideal of education is not merely to prepare people for careers, but even more importantly to mature them as minds and personalities. Someone who develops powers of critical reflection, who by its means sees life and the world more clearly and broadly, who is unafraid of complexities, who can approach the inevitable challenges of life and work with sharp good sense, and who lives therefore with relish because the world is thus made a more brightly lit realm of interest and possibility – such a person has a far better chance of success in all aspects of life.

Helping the education process to produce thinkers – real thinkers, good thinkers – is John L. Taylor's aim in this lucid, compelling and important book. He shows how teaching pupils to apply philosophical styles of thought can achieve the double desiderata of training minds and bringing illumination, depth and perspective to all the subjects in the curriculum. His point about the value of thinking skills is uncontentious and proven. His demonstration of how to bring them to bear across different subjects in the classroom is invaluable. A few lines ago I called this an important book; and it is so because it shows how education can be hugely improved without yet another curriculum reform (although for me a reduction in the number of exams, and a liberation of the curriculum to allow educators to fulfil their vocation properly, remain urgent goals). Taylor offers guidance and techniques which can potentiate the learning experience for students, thereby transforming the value of the existing curriculum by putting its elements into fruitful relationship with each other, offering context and a conceptual framework that makes sense of it all.

The suggestions in the pages that follow come out of educational experience planted in the fertile ground of a philosophical training. John L. Taylor is both a philosopher and a teacher, and his book is itself a demonstration of what it looks like when someone arrives at the goal it wishes education to attain. If there were one highly effective means to improve education without needing extra money or legislation or directives from the Secretary of State, it would be the adoption of the ideas in John L. Taylor's pages. I warmly and indeed urgently recommend them to everyone who cares about our fundamentally important endeavour as educators: they are best hope for a radically better educational future.

A. C. Grayling
London 2011

Acknowledgements

I would like to thank my colleagues at Rugby School, on the Project examining team and on the Perspectives on Science (PoS) development team. I have spent many enjoyable hours discussing education, philosophy and project work with them, and I have learned an enormous amount from them.

I am grateful to Alastair Parvin for sharing his reflections on the informal philosophy classes which I describe in Chapter 1. I am also grateful to all of the students who were happy to be quoted at various points in the book, and to those whose projects I discuss. A special mention here goes to Alex, Bertie and Jonathan for that enjoyable lunchtime talk about the philosophy of sandwiches.

There are a number of people from whom I have learned a great deal about philosophy, and how best it can be taught. I am grateful to my own teachers, particularly Bill Newton-Smith and Roger Teichmann, and to those with whom I have worked during the 12 years that I have been involved in curriculum development. Among these, I would particularly like to thank Michael Reiss, Elizabeth Swinbank and Ralph Levinson. Elizabeth was kind enough to read and comment on the draft text of this book, for which I am very grateful.

I am extremely grateful to Jon Horner for his imaginative and efficient work producing the cartoons. For work on the development of the Philosophy Zone, several conversations from which feature in the coming pages, I would like to thank my colleague Emma Williams and Chris Horne from RM, who provided technical support.

I have had the opportunity of developing most of the ideas I describe in the coming chapters while teaching at Rugby School. I would like to thank Patrick Derham for his long-standing and energetic support of the vision for philosophically richer education, without which many of the initiatives I will be describing would not have been possible.

There are a number of others without whose encouragement this book would not have been written. I am grateful to Mel Wilson and her colleagues at Continuum for their support and assistance. I would also like to thank my family (including in-laws) for their support over many years. Most of all I would like to thank my wife Georgina, to whom this book is dedicated.

Introduction:
The Over-Examined Life

Education should be all about teaching students to think for themselves. But education is being distorted due to an obsession with assessment by examination. Pressure to 'achieve results' means that teaching can turn into spoon-feeding. Instead of being able to excite students with the sheer joy of discovery, teachers feel obliged to focus on training them to jump through assessment hoops.

Would education be better if we spent less time teaching to the test, and more time teaching students to think for themselves? I think it would. I think that education in which the central aim is to equip students to think for themselves is both more enjoyable and more successful. Students who have learned to think for themselves leave education excited about learning and ready for what the rest of life has to bring. And far from this approach causing results to suffer, students who know how to think for themselves will be better equipped to face the challenge that examinations pose.

The question before us, then, is this: how can we find ways to reignite interest in ideas, and foster the ability of students to think, analyse and enquire for themselves? The answer, I will suggest, lies in taking a philosophical approach. Exploring philosophical questions is an excellent way of engaging students and drawing them into more analytical, creative and independent ways of thinking. When I speak about a philosophical *approach*, I mean a way of thinking about concepts and beliefs which can be applied to more or less any subject. It is a matter of adopting a mindset. While formal study of philosophy is obviously helpful, this approach is open to any teacher who is serious about the business of getting their students to think more deeply and independently.

We will explore how a philosophical approach works within the formal curriculum in a range of different subject areas, as well as see how it can be applied fruitfully in informal contexts. I will give examples of 'entry points' which teachers can utilize with their own classes, as well as provide guidance about how best to facilitate philosophical discussions. I will be emphasizing the significant opportunity that project work provides for enabling students to develop their research, analytical and dialectical skills. We will look too at how a philosophical approach can be woven through the whole of the secondary curriculum, and how schools can make it a central component of their ethos by becoming 'Schools of Thought'.

A philosophical approach empowers students to think critically about what they are learning. Philosophy also provides a method which enables greater depth of understanding of the conceptual framework of the knowledge students are acquiring. Its methods are ones which can be applied quite generally. A student can think philosophically about what they are learning in English, the sciences, history, art, geography, and so on. Philosophy can help to provide coherence to an otherwise fragmented curriculum. It offers students space to stand back and think about the big picture. In this way, a philosophical approach serves to counter the atomizing effect of a system of modular examinations, which, by dividing the curriculum into small chunks, and by excluding opportunities for students to consider how different elements of what they are learning relate to each other, tends to discourage the development of a synoptic understanding.

This is a practical book about what can be done, in concrete terms, right now, to create within our schools a more reflective, philosophically literate approach to learning. It is not a book-length moan about the evils of examinations. Nor is it a book full of abstract theory. The main aim of this book is to give hope to teachers who feel that they are trapped by a restrictive assessment regime and have concluded that there is now nothing more to teaching than training students to get through their exams. I want to shine a little light, and point out that that there are pathways along which teachers can go, which lead to a richer, more educationally satisfying approach.

This is also a book in which I lay out how the ideals of the liberal tradition in education can inform and direct the development of the secondary school curriculum. It is thus a challenge both to opponents and advocates of a liberal approach, to 'think again' about what these ideals look like when they are put into practice.

I want to point out ways in which things can be different. The argument I will be making is a simple one: change is possible, and we can demonstrate this by pointing to situations where change is actually happening. There is no need to wait until the curriculum is reformed (again). If we want to take a more philosophical approach – if we want to get students thinking again – we can. This book is all about how we can do it.

Encouraging Self-Sufficiency: How to Liberate Learners through Philosophy

1

Chapter Outline

It makes you think

Early in my teaching career, I was given the opportunity to teach some philosophy to a small group of students. There was a free period on our timetables, and, although we were not working towards an examination, they liked the sound of the subject, and my Head of Department knew that I was keen too.

These lessons were extremely informal. Given the complete absence of a curriculum or assessment regime to tell us what we were supposed to do, we had no further aim than that we should talk about some interesting philosophical questions. Some of these came from the recently released film *The Matrix*. The film is set in a world where humans have their brains connected to a vast computer, which has been programmed by intelligent machines to generate a virtual reality simulation so convincing that it is impossible to tell that it is a mere illusion. The film plays with the sceptical worry that the physical world around us may not be real. Could it all be an elaborate deception? This question, I explained to my students, was not a new one. It goes back to Descartes, often thought of as the founder of modern philosophy, who asked himself whether his sensory experience could be the product of a deception by a malicious, powerful demon: the seventeenth-century equivalent of the evil programmers of *The Matrix*.

Enjoyable as these conversations were, I did wonder about their educational value. They were unstructured. There was no exam to be passed; in fact, I did not use any formal assessment at all. My lesson plans were short, to say the least, on learning objectives. They didn't have a three-point structure, with a nice plenary activity to round off the lesson. We just talked about some interesting philosophical questions. And yet, years later, when one of the students – by then a successful young architect – returned to the school, he told me that what he had learned in those classes had been of more use to him than anything else he had been taught. He found that the opportunity to think freely, and to explore ideas without having to observe strict subject boundaries, had really paid dividends. We were in email contact recently, and he wrote:

> It is rather paradoxical how we never worked towards an exam, and yet I remember far more of it than I do most other subjects I was studying at the time! Of course, the further you get through the education system, the more you realize the contrivance of breaking knowledge up into 'subjects' (especially when our success as a society is arguably now dependent on our ability to do the opposite). I think I was extraordinarily lucky in that I had access to platforms which exposed that contrivance, and gave me the habit of trying to think beyond whatever discipline I happen to find myself in. In the case of architecture and design, that's extremely necessary! Our crash-course conversations through a few centuries of philosophy were a helpful kind of Trojan horse for that, I think.

As a result of my experience of teaching in this way, and seeing the effect it has had on students, I have come to believe that philosophical enquiry – a process of critical, reflective thought which probes questions at a deeper level – is the single most important thing my students and I can engage in. This is for the simple reason that, whatever path they choose to follow in life, they will find that they need the ability to reflect critically and reason clearly about the many questions of life which cannot be answered simply by finding out facts. I also think that life itself is richer and deeper when it is lived in a way which incorporates the reflective dimension. According to Plato, Socrates said that the unexamined life is not worth leading (Plato's *Apology*, 38A). In a different sense, our students lead over-examined lives. This book is about how, in an assessment-driven educational system, some of us have been learning to think once again with our students.

Spoons and hoops

There are many sources of pressure on all of us in education which militate against the development of a more philosophical educational experience, not least among these being the pressure to 'achieve results'. Many of us became teachers because we were inspired by a love of our subject and a desire to equip students with the knowledge and ability to discover the world of learning for themselves. Yet we find ourselves frustrated by the imposition of a curriculum and an assessment structure which seems to squeeze out the scope for creative exploration of ideas, for deep thinking, and for crossing between subject boundaries on journeys of enquiry. The *modus operandi* that we feel obliged to adopt is that of 'teaching-to-the-test'. We all know that our students face assessments which, more than ever before, will determine what options for future work or study are open to them. We would fail them if we didn't give them the best chance to meet the demands of these assessments. And so, with laser-like precision, we hone what we teach to achieve the assessment targets. Teaching is governed by what students need to know to pass their exams. Specifications divide up the world of learning into discrete learning outcomes, so we match this structure in the way we teach, aiming to create the closest correspondence between our lessons and the assessment objectives.

In place of learning about a subject in a free ranging, open-ended way, a way which allows us to explore, enquire and reflect, we end up 'delivering content' (what a ridiculous phrase for the process of teaching!) We spoon-feed our students with 'bite-size chunks' and train them to jump through assessment hoops. It is no coincidence that popular educational websites for students have names like 'bite-size', and that the shelves of high street bookstores are crammed with, well, crammers: books which reproduce the examination syllabus, with colourful pictures and exhortatory notes, enjoining the student to 'Learn this bit . . . .'

As a consequence of the culture of spoon-feeding and hoop-jumping, students fall into the role of passive recipients of the information their teachers ladle into them. Sponge-like, they soak up learning outcomes, and prepare themselves to reproduce these as precisely as possible in their examinations, using the terminology decreed to be acceptable by the examiners.

What is lost, as a result of all this, is the all-important transfer of responsibility for the learning process. By the time our students are aged 18, they ought to be ready for life in the wider world. Whether they go on to higher education or to work, they will be expected to be able to think for themselves. They should not be in constant need of direction. By the time children become adults, they should be self-sufficient, intellectually autonomous individuals, capable of finding things out when they need to know them, and capable of formulating views of their own, which they are able to defend in reasoned discussion and debate.

Yet, instead of becoming more independent as the educational process unfolds, students remain in a state of high dependency. I stopped spoon-feeding my two-year-old daughter for the simple reason that she insisted on grabbing the spoon for herself. However, even into their teenage years, at an age at which, in all other respects, they delight to assert their independence, many students seem quite happy for their teachers to continue to wield the spoons. One said to me, 'We can stop being spoon-fed when we get to university.'

This is not a state of affairs which the universities welcome. A theme of the Nuffield Review of 14–19 Education and Training was the complaint of many admissions tutors that students are arriving at university poorly equipped for the demands of independent learning (Pring et al., 2009). Increasingly, however, one hears of university teachers who, presumably out of desperation, have taken up the spoons, going to great lengths to make their teaching easily digestible for those who have passed through school never learning how to chew things over for themselves.

We will be exploring ways in which a philosophical approach to education can help to counter the trend towards the substitution of real education by spoon-fed training in how to jump through assessment hoops. Philosophy can help both by motivating students to take charge of their learning, and by equipping them with the confidence and skills to begin the all-important processes of critically assessing the information they come across and applying their own judgement in coming to a mature, reflective understanding. For those students and teachers who want to think again, philosophy has much to offer.

Education on a need to know basis

An approach which emphasizes thinking for yourself runs quickly up against the demand – a demand which comes from the students themselves – that what they are taught is what they 'need to know' to pass the exam towards which they are working. 'Is this in the test, sir?', 'Do we need to know this, sir?' These questions indicate that students have well-defined expectations of their teachers, expectations which link directly to the syllabus. What hope, then, is there of adopting a more philosophical approach? Isn't the enterprise doomed to be rejected by the students themselves, who often don't mind being spoon-fed; it is, after all, that little bit easier than having to chew things over?

This reaction from students is partly a reflection of the intense pressure that our contemporary assessment culture places them under. Efforts to achieve a greater degree of autonomy in the classroom, for both students and teachers, run up against the restrictions imposed by a bureaucratic assessment system. One of the effects of this system is that it disconnects the motivation to learn from an appreciation of the intrinsic value of knowledge. Instead of a love of learning for its own sake, the main motivation for students to learn is that they 'need to know' things in order to achieve examination success.

We are never going to get away from the need for some form of assessment, and hence, of ranking. In a competitive marketplace, this means that our keener students will always have at least one eye on the 'market value' of the courses which we teach them. We owe it to our students to help them achieve the best results they can. But this aspiration isn't contradicted by the desire to help them on the path towards autonomy. The two approaches can coexist. In fact, we may go further and point out that by taking a more reflective, philosophical approach, and spending more time encouraging our students to think for themselves, instead of just spoon-feeding them with information, we put them in a better position to do well in their exams, where they will be expected to think on their feet, and will be rewarded for answers which show a greater depth of understanding.

There are practical ways of implementing a conception of philosophical learning which can be made to work *right now* – not when, in some nebulous world of the future, there is a glorious revolution in which all the accreted apparatus of educational bureaucracy dissolves and we emerge into a wide sunlit place, where teachers no longer need to worry about assessment objectives and young people explore the world with all the innocent curiosity of Rousseau's *Emile*.

This book is all about what a viable philosophical approach looks like in practice. We will see that there are opportunities, both within and outside the contemporary curriculum, for engaging in open-ended, creative, deep, reflective philosophical thought. This is true despite the constraints of accountability measures and assessment mechanisms. My main aim is not to moan about the effects of this regime, but to see what we can do with the system we have. We will, however, have cause to comment on whether things might not be improved if some of the infrastructure of accountability through examination results were to be dismantled.

It's good to talk

Among other things, the teenage years are characterized by processes of questioning received wisdom, thinking about identity, wondering how to live and beginning to notice, and question, the difference between the way things appear and the way they really are. It is, then, not coincidental that people often begin to consider the questions of philosophy during their teenage years. This is one reason why introducing teenagers to philosophy can be so effective. They are ready for it. Philosophy gives them permission to question, and puts in their hands the tools with which to begin finding answers for themselves.

Philosophy is best introduced by discussion with students. Talking about some of the fascinating questions which philosophy raises is an excellent way of stimulating students to begin thinking and enquiring for themselves. I find that the majority of students really enjoy lessons where the main aim is simply to discuss a philosophical question. You know that you have hit the mark when the argument continues even after they have left the classroom. Critics might question the value of what is being learned in what might seem to be little more than an unstructured, open-ended chat session. What I emphasize to students, however, is that although they will not be acquiring large amounts of factual knowledge, they will be learning *to do* something, namely, to reason and argue.

One of the many rewarding aspects of working with students in this way is to see their progress over time. Many students are initially nervous and prefer not to say too much. But with careful, gentle encouragement, they grow in confidence and develop their ability to reason well. In a carefully constructed approach, such as we will explore in Chapters 2 and 3, a sequence of philosophical discussions can be structured so as to build up thinking skills of increasing sophistication. In this model, the skills are identified and explicitly taught. As a result, the teacher can help students to think better and, at the same time, draw their attention to the ways in which they are thinking better. This, in turn, gives them the confidence to develop further. Philosophical discussion thus contributes to the development of students' intellectual autonomy. 'It helps us to think', was how one student summed it up, simply but accurately. Students who can reason for themselves, and appreciate the value of being able to do so, are on a path which leads away from spoon-fed dependency and towards intellectual maturity.

Where philosophy begins

We will be exploring steps we can take to transform our schools into places where students develop into more reflective, thoughtful individuals, who are sensitive to the philosophical dimension of everything they learn. Education stands to be immeasurably enriched by an engagement with philosophy, meaning by this an exploration of the 'big' questions which lie at the foundations of each area of educational life.

While there is value in studying philosophy as a discrete subject, much of the most interesting philosophical work that can be done with teenage students begins with critical questioning of the ideas they are learning about in their other subjects of study. So we will focus our attention on the points where philosophy meets other disciplines.

It is not hard to find places across the whole curriculum from which philosophical discussion can begin. All it takes is for the right question to be asked, and a door opens on a new and fascinating world of conceptual puzzles. This can happen during a classroom discussion in an English lesson, or when a student is choosing what to do for an art project. Even something as ordinary as a conversation about what you are having for lunch can be a prelude to philosophy. Here are a few examples of entry points to the world of philosophical enquiry, ranging from the profound to the frivolous:

In English: The mystery of identity

An English class is reading *Hamlet*. After reading the famous soliloquy, the question of personal identity comes up, and the conversation becomes philosophical. Do we have an inner essence – a soul – which determines who we are? Or is identity more fluid? Is it dependent on the roles we choose to play? And what does this mean for those who cannot decide what their role in life is? Is the central tragedy in the play the fact that Hamlet failed to decide who he really was until it was too late? Can that tell us anything about our own lives, and the importance of forming our own identity? The teacher guides the class into a discussion of these questions, and then back to the text, which they examine to see how the play explores the philosophical problem of the self. A group of students enjoys the discussion so much that they decide to do a project in which they research how Shakespeare explores the idea of identity in a number of his plays. Their teacher recommends that they read Colin McGinn's book *Shakespeare's Philosophy* (McGinn, 2006). The students decide to devise and perform a short play featuring a number of Shakespearean characters being interviewed about their life stories on a chat show.

In business studies: The value of a human life

A group of business studies students is thinking about whether every-thing can be assigned an economic value. When decisions are being made about improvements to the safety of the railway network, a mon-etary value is assigned to a single life. What should that value be? Would £ 1,000,000 be about right? Or should we say that the idea of an economic value for life makes no sense? Is life the sort of thing that cannot be given an economic value? If it doesn't make sense to put a value on life, how should we decide how much to spend on rail safety?

In French: The meaning of life

A French class is reading the Albert Camus novel *L'Etranger*. Interpreting this text calls for exploration of the philosophical problem Camus identi-fied using the term 'absurdity'. Where, if not from a transcendent source such as God, is the meaning of life to be found? Can our own quest for meaning in life be illuminated by the strange tale of Meursault, a young man who seemingly throws away an idyllic life? Is Camus implying that life is fundamentally absurd, or is he saying that meaning can be found even in extreme situations, such as that of a young man facing execution for a senseless act of murder?

In physics: The relationship between faith and science

In a physics lesson about the solar system, the teacher introduces a discussion about Galileo and the conflict between science and reli-gion. Suddenly the class has a lot to say. Some of them are convinced that there is perennial opposition between science – which is based on reason and evidence – and religious belief – which is based on faith. Others argue that the two are compatible. The teacher challenges the first group to explain what Galileo meant when he said that the pur-pose of the scriptures is to teach us how to go to Heaven, not how the heavens go. She asks the second group whether they are concerned about the fact that a large percentage of the American population believes that God created humans in their present form, and that evo-lution is false.

In psychology: The problem of free will

A psychology student decides to write a philosophy dissertation on the apparent conflict between science and free will. She has read about experiments which seem to challenge the idea that we make free choices. One set of experiments (by Benjamin Libet) provides evidence of action potentials which start to occur in the brain *prior* to the formation of a conscious decision. Does this show that our sense of free will is an illusion produced by the brain? Her supervisor points her towards further psychological studies, and also suggests that she reads some of the philosophical literature on free will. The student realizes that her question has significant implications for the idea of moral responsibility, and as a result she begins to look at court cases in which evidence of abnormal neurological activity in the defendant's brain has played a part.

In art and design: What is a work of art?

An art student has been to an exhibition at the Tate Modern. She becomes interested in the question, 'What is a work of art?' Her teacher suggests that she researches the work of Marcel Duchamp. This leads her to question whether something becomes a work of art simply by being placed in a gallery. To explore this further, she designs a ceramic vase and photographs it in the kitchen of her home as well as on display on a mantelpiece and in a gallery. She then produces an exhibition of her work and interviews visitors to see how they react to the object in its various settings. She draws her ideas together in an Extended Project, in which she includes her sketchbook, design sheets, research into Duchamp, photographs of her work and an evaluative report in which she reflects on the philosophical link between art and its setting.

Over lunch: The philosophy of sandwiches

It is lunch-time and I am sitting with a group of students. I have returned from the salad bar with a large plate of salad and two slices of bread placed on the opposite edges of my plate. 'I like your sandwich', one of the students remarks. 'But is it a sandwich?' I ask. We spend lunch discussing the concept of a sandwich. A first attempt at a definition is: two pieces of bread with a filling in-between. But do you really need two pieces? Must the filling literally be sandwiched between pieces of bread? Why is an open sandwich still a sandwich, if the 'filling' is in fact a topping? And if you can have a sandwich with just bread and a topping, is cheese on toast a sandwich? What about baguettes – are these sandwiches? Is a kebab a sandwich? The more radical thinkers in the group begin to wonder whether bread is necessary at all. Could there be such a thing as a sandwich without bread? To the surprise of all, post-lunch internet research establishes that one well-known high street food retailer has indeed recently begun selling the 'No-Bread Sandwich'.

The power of projects

Project work provides an ideal vehicle for encouraging creative, independent thought. It is thus highly valuable as an antidote to a curriculum which emphasizes exam-based assessment. Given the constraining effect of question setting and the standardization of acceptable responses which goes on via mark schemes for the majority of examinations nowadays, a clean break is needed if we are to find ways of assessing the sort of creative, deeper, original ways of thinking which happen when students discover the sheer excitement of engaging with philosophy. We need to look beyond the conventional examination if we are to assess capacities such as those of creative thought, in-depth research, sustained development of argument and self-reflective learning.

In the learning model I will be advocating, there are two components: an initial phase of philosophical discussions followed by work on a personal philosophy project. There is a natural link between these elements. Discussion helps to provide ideas for projects, and a personally chosen project provides an opportunity for the student to exhibit their skills in philosophical reasoning.

An advantage of project work is that it offers students the chance to choose for themselves what they want to work on. This has value in helping to motivate students. It is especially appropriate when projects concern philosophical issues. Philosophy is often taught by beginning with the 'great thinkers' of the past. While I would certainly want to encourage engagement with their ideas, I do not think this is the best place to begin when seeking to persuade the average teenager of the value of philosophy. You have to start with questions which have grabbed their imagination. These may be the traditional 'big questions' of philosophy but they may equally well be questions which arise from their wider reading, hobbies, family circumstances, leisure interests or aspirations for future work or study.

Medical ethics

A sixth-form student plans to go on to university to read medicine. As a result of some work experience in a hospital, she becomes interested in exploring the topic of informed consent. Why do we place such importance on asking patients to consent to treatment? What about children? Are they competent to refuse treatment? And what about those who refuse life-saving treatment on religious grounds, such as Jehovah's Witnesses who refuse blood transfusions? She chooses to write an Extended Project on the topic. Her school supervisor suggests that she begins with a study of the history of the change in attitudes, within the medical profession, from a paternalistic approach to one which emphasizes patient autonomy. To provide her with a framework for exploring the ethical and philosophical aspects of the topic, her supervisor also suggests that she reads J. S. Mill's *On Liberty*.

A philosophical curriculum

It is sometimes suggested that philosophical discussion, valuable though it is, should not be part of the formal curriculum. The worry here is that the excitement of philosophical enquiry will be lost if we turn it into an assessed subject. However, given the importance of qualifications as outcomes of the educational process, we cannot get away from the fact that students will give far greater weight to what they learn if it leads to a recognized qualification than they would if they were being invited simply to study something because it is 'good for them'. I think, therefore, that philosophical learning should be assessed and that students should be able to gain qualifications as a result of their work in this area. I will be arguing that philosophical exploration, culminating in project work, should be a part of timetabled teaching in all schools and colleges. There is a good case for saying that all students aged 13–16 should experience an introductory programme of philosophy and project work, and that a similar programme at an advanced level should be available as an option to post-16 students.

Where, you might ask, will we find time for all this? Happily, there is no need to add yet another subject to an already crowded curriculum in order to start teaching this way. There already exists a number of programmes and qualifications which are well suited to a philosophical approach. These include the following:

- The Level 3 Extended Project Qualification
- The Level 2 Higher Tier Project Qualification
- The PoS programme in the history, philosophy and ethics of science
- The International Baccalaureate Theory of Knowledge and Extended Essay
- Programmes for citizenship education
- Religious studies
- Critical thinking.

We will explore ways in which these can be used as cornerstones of a philosophically enriched curriculum. There is a two-way opportunity here: the fact that these qualifications exist provides an opportunity to include more philosophy in the curriculum. And the teaching of these subjects can be enhanced by a more philosophical approach.

This opportunity is not currently being seized as widely as it might be. A recent OFSTED report criticized the way that religious education is sometimes taught without sufficient development of higher-order critical thinking skills (OFSTED, 2010). The same report noted that good practice was to be found when a more philosophical approach was in play. Similarly, citizenship education – a subject which can be taught in a largely didactic fashion – stands to gain tremendously from an infusion of philosophical ideas. We will explore ways in which this can be done.

As well as enriching individual subjects, philosophy can make a contribution to the quality of learning as a whole. Philosophy contributes to *understanding*. To make sense of what they are learning, students need to be able to take a step back from the details and think about the bigger picture.

As a synoptic discipline, which takes as its domain the most general questions of all, philosophy is well placed to assist in this way. We will see how philosophy can serve to 'reunify' the curriculum, allowing students to begin to perceive connections between what they are learning in different subject areas, and giving them a framework for thinking about what it all means.

The philosophical approach which I will be advocating is one which will come naturally to some teachers while leaving others feeling uncomfortable. This may be because they feel that their professional training has not equipped them to engage in this way, or because they are ideologically opposed to this way of doing things. I will be seeking to address both of these concerns. The best way to allay fears about whether this approach can work is by showing how it actually works in practice. The news here is good: this approach has been tried and tested in a wide range of schools, and it has proven possible for teachers of diverse backgrounds to get involved and, supported by carefully constructed resources, begin to move confidently in the new worlds of research facilitation and philosophical mentoring. We will see that many of the criticisms of 'student-centred' approaches, and of 'continuous assessment', can be met provided that the learning model and the method of assessment are carefully designed to pre-empt many of the common problems with coursework-based approaches.

Theory and practice

This is a book about teaching and philosophy, and how the two relate. Philosophy has a reputation for being an abstract, irrelevant discipline. So I should make clear that, in calling for a more philosophical approach to teaching, I am not suggesting that we should engage in a great deal of abstract theorizing. Talk about deeper, more analytic, reflective, independent learning is fine, but it will carry little weight with most teachers unless it is clear that these ideals can be realized in the classroom. It is all very well having lofty aspirations for a philosophically richer way of educating, but whatever else a philosophical approach means, it *must be teachable*.

As someone whose full-time job is teaching, I am as keen as anyone to find ways of making sure that a philosophical approach to

Figure 1.1 The see-saw of theory and practice

teaching actually works. But as someone who has spent much of the past 12 years thinking about education from a philosophical standpoint, I can see that there is an opposing risk too. It is easy to lose sight of our educational ideals in the midst of the pressures of actually getting lessons taught. We can become too concerned with achieving the immediate targets we have been set, and stop thinking about why and how we are actually teaching. We can lose sight of the bigger picture.

What we need is a good balance of philosophical theory and peda-gogical practice. Unfortunately, due to the fact that philosophy is often dismissed as abstract and irrelevant, we tend not to get the balance right. Philosophy is not given enough weight. The result is that our teaching stays stuck on the ground, and our ideals stay up in the air (see Figure 1.1).

Teaching philosophically is about taking a pragmatic approach, in which we work out our ideals during a process of reflective practice. Theory and practice have to engage each other in a dynamic interplay. We try ideas out in the classroom and then we reflect on how things went. We evaluate our teaching in the light of a philosophical under-standing of what really matters. In this way, philosophical ideas can help to lift the way we teach, and practical classroom experience can help to bring lofty philosophical ideals back down to earth.

The liberal ideal

This book is chiefly about practical steps which can be taken in order to enrich education through exploration of its philosophical dimension. But it is also about philosophical ideals. I expect that you will by now have discerned where my own philosophical sympathies lie. I am an unashamed advocate of liberal education. I will not dwell at length on the theme that our educational system badly needs to rediscover the riches of its liberal tradition, as this case has already been made eloquently (Derham and Worton, 2010; Nussbaum, 2010). But before we get down to looking in more detail at what actually works in the classroom, I will round out these introductory remarks with a brief statement of why I think that we need to rediscover education's liberal roots, and how philosophy can help here.

Our educational practices ought to reflect the philosophy and values which underpin liberal democracy. They ought to place high store on the goals of fostering intellectual autonomy, respect for diverse opinions and the commitment to use rational enquiry as the means by which to pursue truth and negotiate disagreement. In short, a liberal democracy ought to prize and promote a liberal educational system.

What characterizes the liberal approach is its understanding of the end of the educational process. A properly functioning educational system will yield autonomous young adults: people with the ability and disposition to think for themselves; to reflect on matters in a critical, evaluative manner, reaching conclusions which can be justified in the light of the evidence and the balance of the arguments put before them.

Why do we really need liberal education? In economically straitened times, it may seem more than enough simply to aim at employability. The need, however, relates to things more fundamental than economic prosperity. Liberal education is required to sustain the foundations of civil society. A healthy democracy requires individuals who have learned to think for themselves and know how to manage their disagreements with others by means of rational discussion, not coercion or manipulation.

We should, therefore, be concerned that there are many pressures on students which militate against the development of intellectual autonomy. We need to address the fact that the educational culture of teaching-to-the-test encourages passivity and dependency, instead of active autonomy. This is not just a pedagogical problem: it is a problem with social and political implications.

Critics of liberalism often accuse it of an excessive focus on the individual, to the detriment of a concern with the well-being of society. No man is an island, the argument goes. If our philosophy of education privileges individual autonomy, are we not in danger of undermining the fabric of the society within which individuals exist? Isn't there a need to strike a balance between individual freedom of thought and respect for the constraints that are necessary for the integration of individuals into a community?

The debate about liberalism is not one which need detain us here. There is no necessary tension between the promotion of the goal of individual intellectual autonomy and the wider goal of education, namely, that of providing a foundation for civil society. There would be a problem only if the rights of the individual and the needs of society are opposed to each other. But I don't think that this is the case at all. On the contrary, educating individuals really well is one of the best things we can do to create a stronger society. If we are concerned to promote social health and the growth of a vibrant civic society, we should care about the education of the individual. It is by ensuring that each individual is given a chance to engage imaginatively with the perspectives of others that they will learn the civic virtues. This is the sort of engagement which a subject like philosophy is well equipped to facilitate.

We are discussing no small matter, said Socrates, but how we ought to live (Plato, *Republic*, Book 1:352d). Whatever else we might say in answer, it was clear to Socrates that a good life must be a reflective life: the unexamined life is not worth living. Equipping the young with the capacity for reflection is essential as a means of promoting human well-being. Reflective individuals know how to make use of experience as a guide in navigating life's narrower passages. They have learned to consider another person as another self; to recognize the demands that the humanity of others places on their own conduct. In these ways, they have learned much that contributes towards well-being. Education which fails to foster the disposition towards reflective enquiry thereby fails in a fundamental way. A philosophical approach is not an optional extra, but is an essential component of an education which aims to help young people develop into intellectually autonomous, reflective, sensitive individuals. It is for this reason that it has an essential contribution to make to education in a liberal democracy.

Socratic Mentoring: A Guide to Philosophical Approaches to Learning

2

Chapter Outline

The examination of your life

At the heart of ancient Athens was the agora: a large space in the city where people would come to trade both goods and ideas. Sitting in the shade under the 'stoa' (the porticoes which surround the edge of the agora, and from which we get the name of one of the major schools of ancient Greek philosophy, the Stoics) you could engage your fellow citizens in conversation about matters of politics, commerce or philosophy.

Socrates spent many of his days in the agora of Athens, where he became famous for openly engaging the Athenian citizens in philosophical discussion. In educational terms, the setting would be called 'informal'. There was no syllabus and there were no written examinations to be passed. Yet you could be sure that a conversation with Socrates would be educational in a deep and quite probably life-changing way.

Instead of an examination of your subject knowledge, an encounter with Socrates became an examination of your life. Socrates wanted to know how people understood the ideas – such as justice and courage – upon which they based their lives. This was no merely academic exercise. Socrates was well aware that people live, and some die, for their ideas – and that it was, therefore, of the first importance that these ideas should be examined closely.

Socrates was a passionate seeker after truth. As told by Plato, in his account of Socrates' trial, a trial which culminated in his fellow Athenians sentencing him to death for the crimes of corrupting the youth and abandoning the gods of the state, Socrates tells the story of how his friend Chaerephon had gone to Delphi to ask a question of the oracle. 'Who is the wisest man?' Chaerephon asked – to which the oracle replied that there was none wiser than Socrates. This answer puzzled Socrates for many years, since he did not consider himself wise at all. How then could he be the wisest of men? Eventually, he realized that, unlike many others who laid claim to knowledge when in fact they were ignorant, he was truly wise, because he did not think that he knew things that he did not know (*Apology*, 21d).

To be a philosopher is to be, literally, a lover of wisdom. Socrates came to understand his role as a teacher of philosophy in terms of helping people to see the limitations of their 'knowledge'. His was not a dogmatic style of teaching. He did not have a body of doctrines to convey. Instead, he wanted to question, to probe and to challenge the things people tended to say when asked questions like, 'What is justice?' or 'Is virtue something that can be taught?' In these conversations, he employed the method of drawing out people's ideas by asking a series of critical questions. This inquiry had a specific aim. Socrates wanted to show people

Figure 2.1 The Socratic gadfly

that they did not know what they thought they did. He called himself 'the gadfly', seeing it as his role to sting the city of Athens – which he likened to a lazy horse – into greater thoughtfulness as well as intellectual humility (Figure 2.1).

In this chapter, I am going to be recommending that we follow Socrates' example. Teaching philosophically should happen by a process I call 'Socratic mentoring', in which, like Socrates, we probe and challenge our students, questioning the things they say, and stimulating the intellectually somnolent to begin thinking for themselves.

Waking up to philosophy

Immanuel Kant famously remarked that reading the philosophy of David Hume helped him to wake from his dogmatic slumbers. In some philosophical discussions, you can see students wake up right in front of your eyes.

It is a Tuesday afternoon in the Philosophy Zone, a place where 16- and 17-year-old students from schools in the town where I teach gather to discuss philosophy. We meet for 45 minutes. There is very little didactic teaching. We meet simply in order to talk about a philosophical question. The sessions are part of a teaching programme which is designed to lay foundations for subsequent project work. The projects which students go on to write often address philosophical themes.

Today, we are talking about the problem of other minds. How do we know that other people have minds? We normally think that we can tell what other people are thinking by the way they behave. To challenge this idea, I put the 'zombie' thought experiment to the group. Imagine, I tell them, that there is a race of zombies: creatures just like ordinary human beings, as far as we can tell from their behaviour – but entirely lacking in conscious awareness. When we interact with these people, their behaviour gives every impression that they are conscious – they walk around, talk, observe and respond to the world just as if they were conscious. But inside their minds, there is no 'inner light' of conscious self-awareness. They are acting and reacting with no sensation of what they are doing. They give every impression to an outside observer that they are conscious. But in fact, they are not conscious at all.

The zombie thought experiment is a troubling one. It forces us to question the strength of the link between the behavioural evidence and the internal reality of another person's mind. The question I put to the Philosophy Zone group is: 'What reason do you have for thinking that the other people around you *aren't* zombies? You can never see inside the mind of someone else. You don't know what their stream of conscious experience is like. How can you be sure that they even have conscious experiences?'

Conversation ranges around this extraordinary idea. Some of the more perceptive students begin to question the terms of the thought experiment. Do these zombies see things? Their behaviour suggests they do. If they can point out the colours in a flower, or duck when a ball is thrown at their heads, we can scarcely avoid describing them as creatures that see. The initial distinction between behaviour and mental life may be closer than was originally imagined.

But then the discussion comes closer to home. We move from the world of imaginary thought-experiments to the real world of scientific enquiry. I tell the group about a remarkable experiment which has been conducted on apparently comatose patients by scientists in Cambridge. They have found that they can communicate with a patient who has been diagnosed as being in a 'persistent vegetative state', by asking him questions while his brain is being scanned in a magnetic resonance imaging machine. The patient answers by exciting different regions of his brain. This is the opposite situation to the one described in the story about the Zombies. Here is someone whose behaviour suggests he is not conscious – but perhaps, in some sense, he still is.

Discussions like these really create a buzz. They are exciting and disturbing. They make students wake up and start thinking. They are a sort of philosophical wake-up call. Once the discussion starts to flow, students begin to realize that it is easier in philosophy to raise questions than it is to come up with answers. Suddenly, a lot of things which seemed certain start to appear uncertain. Some students find this uncertainty and openness exciting. They realize that the fact that the question is open means that there is a chance for them to develop ideas of their own. But others begin to wonder what the point of such discussion is. What is the point of having a conversation, if no-one knows the answers? To answer this objection, we need to think about the character of philosophical discussion.

Talking for real

When I open a philosophical discussion by asking students whether we know what is going on inside someone else's mind, I am asking a *genuine* question. I am not totally sure of the answer. I do have an opinion – I am not a complete agnostic. But I am not sure. And this means that the conversation I am about to have with the class is a real discussion. We are exploring a topic about which there is real uncertainty. The question is not just a rhetorical ploy.

The reality of the discussion is a distinguishing feature of classroom philosophical conversation. What do I mean by that? Well, consider the many non-genuine conversations which go on everyday in our classes. We play a game of 'let's pretend the teacher doesn't really know the answer . . .' So, for example, if I am teaching a physics class, I might say something like, 'I wonder what will happen to this ping-pong ball when I place it on top of this hair-dryer and switch the hair-dryer on?' Here, I am engaged in a pretence of not knowing what will happen. My question is meant to invite someone in the class to say, 'It will get blown away', and someone else to say, 'It will hover in mid-air.' The second response is in fact the correct answer, and I knew this when I asked the question, but I will keep up the pretence, and say, 'That's interesting. Why do you think that?' I might even challenge the student who has given the right answer ('Surely not? How could it possibly hover?') in order to test to see how confidently he can back up his hypothesis.

None of my questions are genuine. I know the answer I am looking for. I am not really engaged in an enquiring discussion with the class. I am *pretending* to enquire, as a way of helping the group come to appreciate the particular point of physics which I am about to demonstrate to them. My 'wondering' is an act, as is my 'doubting' the correct answer.

This is all part of the harmless repertoire of classroom drama. I am playing a role – the role of the innocent enquirer, one who does not know, and is making guesses, and testing them out. But in fact, I do know (or at least, am fairly confident about) what will happen when I do the test.

The situation when we come to philosophical discussion is quite different. Here, the whole point is that we are opening up questions to which there are no agreed answers. Nobody knows for sure. This feature of philosophy – the fact that it deals in uncertainties – is one of the things that sets it apart from other subjects. Philosophy is what we begin to do after we have established the facts. It involves taking a look beyond them, to try to see a pattern. It involves thinking about what the facts mean, how we come to know them and whether we really know what we think we do. By its very nature, then, it involves speculative thought.

In educational terms, the speculative character of philosophy presents a challenge. It is a challenge for the teacher, who has to accept that they have entered a realm where they do not have the answers. This is something which can be quite unsettling for teachers who feel that their authority rests on their subject knowledge. How can you teach, if you don't know the answers? It is also a challenge for students, who can quickly begin to feel lost, as questions mount up, and there seem to be no secure answers.

As a rule, few people find it easy to live with uncertainty. Instead of honestly accepting that the evidence is sometimes ambiguous, people tend to counter doubt by dogmatically reasserting their own point of view. This was a tendency which Hume commented upon:

> The greater part of mankind are naturally apt to be affirmative and dogmatical in their opinions; and while they see objects only on one side, and have no idea of any counterpoising argument, they throw themselves precipitately into the principles, to which they are inclined; nor have they any

indulgence for those who entertain opposite sentiments.
(Hume, 1910, XII.3)

People tend to see one side of the argument only. In order to preserve treasured certainties, they build up barriers against any ideas which pose a challenge to their dogmatically held beliefs. In this fact, we see the origin of much of the divisive behaviour which stems from misplaced conviction.

Philosophy can help. It can teach us to live with uncertainty. Through enquiring into the foundations of knowledge, and learning to recognize its limits, we can come to appreciate something about the true nature of the human condition. It is this gain in self-knowledge which Socrates called 'wisdom'. With it goes an appreciation of the fact that we cannot simply dismiss out of hand the beliefs of those who disagree with us. None of us enjoys the privilege of knowing, for sure, that we are right. An encounter with philosophy, therefore, engenders a degree of openness to the opinions of others; it teaches us humility. When students ask about the point of discussing questions to which we do not know the answers, you can truthfully reply that they are learning one of life's most important lessons. They are learning to live with uncertainty.

Openness to counter-argument

If we accept the possibility that our philosophical beliefs may be mistaken, then we will take seriously the arguments of those who disagree with us. Openness to counter-argument is one of the hallmarks of a rational enquirer, and it is one of the main attributes which philosophical discussion should help to develop in students. We will explore this in some depth, and apply it both within our model for philosophical discussion, and as a central point in teaching and assessing the quality of a student's writing about philosophical questions.

Oliver Cromwell once beseeched the Presbyterian Church in Scotland to 'consider that you might be mistaken'. The reply came back: 'Would you have us be sceptics in matters of religion?' And so what could have been a peaceably resolved disagreement became a pretext for war. Intransigence in matter of belief, taken together with the fact of disagreement about fundamentals, makes a potent and dangerous cocktail. One of the best lessons to take away from a basic introduction to philosophy is the realization that, however certain your convictions, subjective certainty does not imply truth. You may be mistaken. The probability of disagreement turning into conflict is lowered if dogmatic certainty is tempered by this recognition.

A degree of humility is lacking in those who think it impossible that they are wrong. People who believe that they possess absolutely certain knowledge will have little interest in having philosophical discussions with those who hold differing views. In the same way that my 'discussion' in the physics lesson lacked authenticity, a teacher of dogmatically held beliefs is not going to engage truly in philosophical discussion with his or her students. The students themselves will recognize this, and sense that talk about 'thinking critically', in the mouth of such a teacher, is a matter of rhetoric. Recognition of the fallibility of all claims to knowledge of the real world is a presupposition of effective philosophical education.

We have noted that a consequence of this fallibility is that the teacher becomes a genuine participant in the conversation. For who knows? Something could be said by a student which makes the teacher think again. This is one of the reasons why philosophical discussion in the classroom is so dynamic. Teachers join in the conversation as seekers after the truth, accepting that their students might well see some points more clearly than they do. When it comes to Socratic mentoring, the process goes both ways.

The art of articulacy

We all learn all the time from things which are said during conversations. Discussion has a life and accessibility which marks it out from both textual forms of learning and didactic discourse. It is a natural context within which learning can happen. One of the things which students can learn through philosophical discussion is the art of articulacy. Participation in philosophical discussion helps them develop the ability to articulate thoughts about fundamental matters.

It may seem odd that we should have to teach teenagers how to be articulate. Don't they have plenty to say for themselves? But articulating *ideas* is not something which comes naturally to most people, whether they are teenagers or not. This is particularly so when the ideas concern abstract questions of philosophy. Students need to learn how to express thoughts in a personal yet academically credible way. This learning happens through participation in conversation. You cannot learn articulacy from a textbook.

As a transferable skill, articulacy is of enormous importance. Throughout life, key opportunities will hinge on how confident and capable someone is at expressing their ideas or arguing for their point of view. The value of oral communication in a strongly networked world is greater than ever. This is a further reason why it is important to give students the opportunity to develop their ability to articulate ideas during philosophical conversation in the classroom.

Developing articulacy

Developing articulacy is a matter of developing confidence within students – the confidence to add their own ideas to the discussion, and to take the risk of having those ideas subjected to critical questioning and examination. This is not something which many students feel naturally confident in doing. Articulacy is an attribute which needs fostering.

Seminar discussions of philosophical questions provide an excellent setting for helping students grow in confidence when speaking about ideas. In a programme of ethical and philosophical enquiry, I would normally run a few sessions in which everybody is welcome to contribute, but where there is no expectation that everyone will. This way, quieter members of the group can settle in and learn by listening to others. But at some point, all of them should say something. So an exercise can be inserted into the programme which will require everyone in the group to speak.

A low-key way of doing this is by asking each group member to interview someone else – a friend, a family member, a teacher or even a suitable member of the public – about their beliefs on a philosophical topic. In the PoS course, there is a lesson exploring the question 'What came before the Big Bang?' This question works well in an interview setting. Students are asked to write a short series of questions and carry out an interview. They are then asked to present the opinions of the person who they interviewed to the rest of the group (it may be necessary here to address the issue of anonymity; if the person interviewed wishes to remain anonymous, that wish should be respected).

The value of this exercise is that every student is expected to speak – but they are not yet being asked to venture their own views. This makes joining the conversation that little bit easier. When facilitating this activity, you can exercise your judgement about whether to take the discussion further into argument ('That's an interesting idea – would anyone here want to support what that person believes?'; 'Can anyone think of a counter-argument to what we've just heard?') You may want to do this as a way of helping the more confident members of the group to put forward their own ideas as well as reviewing those of others.

Round-table discussion

There is something democratic about discussion. People involved in discussion approach a topic, in some sense, as peers. This democratic feeling should be reflected in the organization of the classroom space. So it pays to give thought to the physical setting for a discussion session.

I had the opportunity, a few years ago, of redesigning a classroom. I planned to use this room for philosophical seminars, and in an ideal world I would have liked there to be a round table in the room. As it happened, the room's dimensions did not allow this, and we had to settle for an oval table. The room was christened 'The oval room', and the students were called 'Philosophers of the oval table'.

What I liked about teaching in the oval room was that I could sit *with* the students. I was not standing in front of them, or even sitting behind a desk, gazing out at them as they sat in serried ranks before me. I was next to them. My position in the room was chosen to send a very clear message: when it comes to philosophy, the only authority is the authority of reasoned argument. It would be disingenuous to pretend that we were equals: I had the benefit of having studied philosophy for more years than they had lived. But that fact alone did not place me above contradiction, and if they could come up with a better argument than I could, then I could not correct them by saying, 'Trust me: I am the teacher – I know best.' In the sense, then, that no-one starts from a pre-sumed position of authority, philosophical discussion is a democratic affair and the teacher, while they may be a guide, is certainly not a sage.

For the teacher setting out to engage the class in Socratic dialogue, it is, therefore, worth giving consideration to the question of classroom layout. Being seated with the students sends a message about the fact that the teacher is also an enquirer after the truth. At the same time, the teacher has a responsibility which students do not: to ensure that the standards of the discussion are upheld. I will sometimes create a large circle (with or without an oval table), in which I will sit alongside students, but with a slightly wider gap between myself and the rest of the group. Or I might 'choose' a slightly higher chair for myself. This position affords the advantages of an open, participatory, seminar feel, while at the same time quietly sending the message (if it is not already clear) that the teacher will be keeping charge of the overall flow of the conversation.

Ground-rules for philosophical discussion

Once discussion is about to begin, some ground-rules need to be clearly understood. There are conventions which govern any class-room discussion, and it may be appropriate to remind students of these. The class can be asked to draw up its own code of conduct for philosophical discussion. They should, with a little prompting, be able to come up with points such as 'One person talks at a time', 'Don't make personal attacks on others', 'Don't be intentionally offensive' and 'Respect others' opinions'. If the topic is a sensitive one, the 'Chatham House' rule – that the identity of those who express views in the con-versation should not be disclosed outside the group – may also need to be introduced.

Conventions such as these should be in play in any classroom discus-sion, and the teacher will need to be ready to enforce them, gently but firmly. It is important that the members of the group feel secure. They will gain that feeling if they sense that although free exchange of ideas is allowed, there are limits to what is appropriate.

The place for passion

Participants in philosophical discussions are being invited to discuss topics about which they may well have deep feelings. And given the fact that philosophical questions are essentially contestable, the subject matter will often be controversial. There will be divergent views among the group, and the argument will at times be passionate. This is not something which the teacher should shy away from. On the contrary, the best discussions are often those in which there is a clash between strongly held positions. This point was made by the authors of a Research Study on the Perspectives on Science Course:

> Diversity, passionate advocacy and positioning of extreme points of view are characteristics of good discussion. While passion and extreme points of view can sometimes appear intimidating to other students, teachers ought not to be unduly worried; indeed such characteristics can be harnessed for productive discussion. (Levinson et al., 2008, p. 30)

One reason why teachers might worry about things getting heated is that what should be a reasoned argument will turn into a quarrel. But this need not happen, so long as the discussion is properly managed. One of the great benefits which philosophy has to offer to education is that it provides a model of how people who hold radically opposed beliefs can still engage rationally and learn from each other. I have sat through many exchanges between professional academic philosophers, and one of the most impressive things is to see that such discussions are normally motivated by a sincere concern to find out the truth. The exchanges may be passionate, but it is understood that the purpose of criticizing an argument is to help determine where the truth lies – not to score points at someone else's expense.

However, philosophical argument can appear downright rude to people who have been brought up to believe that whatever someone says sincerely is immune to criticism. There is a view which abjures rational, critical reflection entirely. Proponents of relativism argue that virtues such as respect and tolerance imply that people have a 'right to their opinion', so that the activity of countering someone's expressed philosophical beliefs is a little like telling them that their dress sense is appalling. Belief is a personal matter, so criticism of belief is bound to be taken personally.

By way of response, I would cite Mary Geach: 'the way to show respect for a sage is to accept his teaching, but the way to respect a philosopher is to argue' (Geach and Gormally, 2005, p. xxi). To argue back is to take what someone says *seriously*. It shows *more* respect to treat someone's beliefs as worthy of discussion than merely to nod supinely, and mutter 'whatever works for you'.

It is important, therefore, to be quite clear with students from the outset that they should expect that what they say will be listened to, but that they should also expect that there will be debate – and this will involve criticism of their opinions by others. The purpose of philosophical argument should be explained. Students need to appreciate that the goal is to pursue truth – not to humiliate or embarrass people, and certainly not to use the fact that the discussion will be argumentative as an excuse for making personal attacks on others.

Setting the stage

Our goal is to have rich, enjoyable discussions, in which students actively contribute their own ideas and arguments in response to a philosophical question. The teacher takes the role of Socratic mentor – the 'guide at the side, not the sage on the stage' (a phrase first coined by American Professor of Education, Alison King). It is all about facilitating the flow of the discussion: providing the occasional gentle nudge, playing Devil's advocate from time to time, prompting students to reflect more deeply when important ideas come up and suggesting new avenues for enquiry when the present phase of the conversation looks like it has run its course.

That is what we want to see happening. But there is always that frightening moment, after the students have assembled, the teacher has set the scene and the philosophical stimulus question has been asked, when silence descends. Who will pick up the ball and run with it? What if no-one says anything? This is the moment at which the faith of the philosophical teacher is tested. If the silence is prolonged, or the contributions from the group are brief and reluctant, there is a real temptation to give up on philosophical dialogue and revert to 'chalk and talk'.

At such times, it is important to have faith in the power of philosophical questions. To a nervous teacher, silence may be interpreted as an indication that things aren't working. After all, the whole point is to have a *discussion*. But silence can equally well betoken real thought and be the precursor to a really interesting and stimulating conversation in which the students offer ideas which they have first turned over in their own minds. The question we need to explore is: how can we create the conditions which make such discussions possible?

The conversations which do work well are usually very carefully planned. Appearances can be deceptive. It may look as though the Socratic mentor in the group is doing very little – just issuing the odd remark here and there, while the students are actively involved in discussing and debating for themselves. But you can be quite sure that a great deal of stage-setting will have gone on to make this possible. To get philosophical discussion going in the classroom is a genuinely difficult teaching challenge. There are all sorts of ways in which it can go wrong. It takes skill and experience on the part of the teacher to set things up so as to enable successful discussion to flow freely and, even then, there are no guarantees that what follows the initial awkward silence will be really good philosophical discussion. We are dealing with teenage students, for whom what happens in the classroom is just one part of a whole kaleidoscope of pieces that make up their complicated lives. There will be days when even the keenest don't feel in the mood to talk philosophy.

Any lesson can go astray on account of troubled tempers or the intrusion of an untimely wasp, but during lessons in which the teacher is deliberately letting go of the reins and expecting the class to take a more active, responsible role, there are even more potential pitfalls than usual. Add to that the fact that, when we are considering questions of philosophy, we are opening up issues which are personal, and for some students, may be extremely sensitive, and you can see why classroom management of philosophical discussion poses a real teaching challenge.

The seeds of success – or failure – of philosophical discussions are sown at the planning stage. So what are the conditions which give us the best chance of success? One promising starting point is a well-chosen, interesting question.

Questions of interest

We are expecting students to contribute their own ideas. Students are far more likely to do this if the chosen question is one which they find interesting. If the question interests them, it is more likely that they will have given some thought to it and have views about how it should be answered. This means that the conversation is more likely to get off to a good start.

It may seem too obvious to need saying, but there are plenty of philosophy courses which begin in a totally abstract way and fail to make any connection to the lives of the students. This won't do at all if the aim is to start a discussion. Students need to be motivated to participate. A question which has been carefully chosen to grab their interest will help to create the motivation for them to start talking.

Teachers should not assume that the philosophical questions they find most fascinating are the ones which will grip the students. A teacher might think that Kant's transcendental deduction of the categories is the best thing since sliced bread. But if her students don't share her affection for idealistic metaphysics, this will not be a good place to start the conversation.

I learned this lesson for myself when writing materials for the philosophy lessons in the PoS course. The first version of these materials was based heavily on the things I had been taught in my university course. That turned out to be a mistake. The material was too demanding for the average 16-year-old student, but more importantly, the questions I was writing about simply weren't the ones in which my students were interested.

I am not suggesting that student interest is the *only* criterion for inclusion in a programme of study. There are some central topics which simply have to be taught, regardless of how interesting they are. But when looking at ways of getting discussion going, it really does matter that the questions are linked to the students' world.

Learning which questions work is, therefore, something which requires a working knowledge of the interests of students. Many of these questions are connected to our basic interest in ourselves. It is human nature to find human nature interesting, and students are no exception to this rule. In the United Kingdom, the second most popular Advanced Level qualification for post-16 students is psychology. Why? If you look on a student chat forum, the answer is clear. Students find the questions really interesting, because, ultimately, they are questions about human nature. We are asking questions because we want to make sense of the mystery of our own selves. This might sound a little narcissistic, but it is a motivation of which Socrates would have approved. One of the quotations found inscribed in the Temple of the Delphic Oracle read: 'Know thyself'. And as Pope added: 'Presume not god to scan. The proper study of mankind is man' (Pope, 1870, p. 225). It does no harm at all to look for a human interest angle when getting discussion started.

Good discussion starters

Are there ghosts?
Should we research on human embryos?
Should we allow cloning of human beings?
Does homeopathy work?
Is the universe designed?
What came before the big bang?
Could there be a thinking machine?
Do we have free will?
What would make an advertisement unethical?
Do we have souls?
Is beauty in the eye of the beholder?
Am I the same person that I was when I was born?
Should we allow screening of embryos for genetic defects?
Should euthanasia be legal?
Is the mind the same as the brain?
Could you survive the death of your body?
Does my dog dream?
Do my genes determine my destiny?
Do other people see colours in the same way that I do?
Is science replacing religion?

Questions about the human mind, about nature and nurture, about fate and free will, about our souls and our bodies, about our place in the universe, about whether the universe was designed with us in mind, about our relation to other animals and about how we ought to live, especially questions of life and death – these are some of the questions which stand a good chance of grabbing the interest of teenage students.

Even some of the questions which seem to be counter-examples to my rule about human interest turn out to have links to human concerns. So, for instance, the question about the existence of an intelligent designer is a question about whether a being somewhat like us is behind the universe as a whole. And the question of whether my dog dreams is a question about whether we are inescapably anthropomorphic in the way that we think about non-human animals: are we projecting what we know about our own minds onto creatures who are in fact quite different? Many of the questions of philosophy are, in part, questions about ourselves; hence their perennial fascination.

The things they say

The opening phase of a philosophical discussion needs some orchestration. One of the most important roles of the Socratic mentor is to guide students to the right place from which to start. Aristotle advised that the place to begin, when you are addressing a philosophical problem is with a survey of the 'endoxa': the common beliefs or opinions of those who have thought about the problem. Received wisdom may not be right, but at least it provides something to start talking about. By giving your students a brief introductory look at the spectrum of opinion on a question, you are providing them with a chance to make an informed choice about where they would situate themselves. They will be made aware of ideas they would never have thought of for themselves. They will also have a sense of which views they disagree with, and, therefore, need to argue against, once they have decided where on the spectrum of belief they stand. It is the job of a good guide to give an idea of the lie of the land. A survey of the endoxa is a way of helping to sketch the contours of the intellectual landscape.

There is a further educational advantage to beginning with a survey of the endoxa. Most students are much more comfortable when they are reviewing what other people have said or thought than they are in articulating and defending views of their own. It is difficult to be original, and it is especially daunting to venture your own ideas in a setting where you run the risk of being exposed to counter-argument. We need to give students the courage and confidence to do this. But at an early stage in their exposure to philosophical discussion, we will simply want them to start talking about philosophy. And they will be more likely to do this if they are invited to talk about what someone else has said or thought. It is a slightly more secure way into what, for many, can be an exciting but quite daunting way of learning.

Philosophical lego

When initiating a philosophical discussion, it is valuable to make the first item an exercise in surveying what informed people have to say about the topic to be discussed. It is rather like emptying lego blocks onto the table for the children to play with. Once they have had a look at what ideas and arguments are out there, they can begin selecting pieces and working with them – assembling some, pulling others apart, discarding yet others. Philosophical discussion needs skill – but it does also need content. This can come from many sources:

- Brainstorming with the group to elicit their first thoughts on the question under discussion
- Reading an extract from the writings of a philosopher
- Taking extracts from a blog discussion of a philosophical question
- Reading a newspaper opinion piece together
- Inviting one group member to present a précis of an article introducing the question
- Interviewing members of the public then presenting their views
- Researching and presenting real-life case studies which raise philosophical issues
- Telling a story (Plato used myths to introduce philosophical ideas)
- Giving a brief overview of how an idea has changed over time (a genealogical account).

The centrality of ethics

There are good reasons for introducing ethical questions at an early stage in a programme of philosophical discussion. Ethics is that branch of philosophy in which we address the question of how we ought to live. As Socrates remarked (in Plato's *Republic*, Book 1:352d), this is no small matter. Given its centrality in the whole of life, ethics ought to figure centrally in education. We might even say that education is an induction into ethical life. The educated person is someone who knows how to answer the Socratic question about how we ought to live. Everything we teach should play a part in enabling students to become informed, sensitive, critically aware, and, ultimately, capable of making reasoned judgements about things that matter.

At the pedagogical level as well, there is a strong case for the introduction of ethics. Ethical topics provide excellent starting points for discussion and debate. Set alongside other branches of philosophy, ethical questions work well as discussion starters because of their ubiquity. We engage in ethical argument whenever an evaluative question is posed. What should I wear? How should I spend my money? Was that movie any good? These questions, which relate to matters of value, are ethical in character. Reasoning about such questions constitutes a significant part of all the reasoning we do.

Ethical discussion usually works extremely effectively in the classroom. Students care about topics such as the ethics of animal welfare, or media portrayal of the female body. They are more likely to have opinions of their own, which they tend to be more ready to offer and defend, than on most other philosophical questions. Moreover, the nature of ethical subjects means that the topics are inherently contentious. There will usually be a spread of views, all of which can be defended to at least some degree, and this helps to make for a livelier discussion. It means that the importance of learning to recognize and respond to opposing viewpoints can readily be taught.

Since ethics is concerned with how we ought to live, almost any topic will have an ethical aspect to it. It therefore becomes possible to bring any subject which interests the student into the realm of philosophical discourse. For younger teenage boys, for instance, making a connection between philosophy and football may be the best option for the Socratic mentor looking to get the ball rolling with philosophical discussion.

Philosophy and football

Your enthusiasm for Socratic mentoring is rewarded. Not, like your illustrious forebear, with a cup of hemlock. Instead you have been timetabled to teach an enrichment lesson on a Friday afternoon to a bottom set of 15–16-year-old students. The group happens to be mainly made up of boys whose interests do not go much wider than football. How, you think, can I engage them with philosophy?

You could let them know that the famous French existentialist philosopher Albert Camus was a goalkeeper. Or you could show them a clip from Monty Python's 'Philosophy Football Match'. Wisely, you dismiss these ideas and start to think instead about whether you could get the students thinking and arguing. One promising approach is to explore some ethical questions linked to the way in which sport has developed, such as the following:

- Has football been ruined by the vast amount of money it generates (at least for certain clubs)?
- Should we have fewer foreign players in the UK league?
- What should be done to professional sportsmen who use performance enhancing drugs?

You find that (a) your students know a fair bit (b) they have opinions and (c) they are quite happy to discuss these. You have made a start in engaging the class in discussion of an ethical topic. Where do you go next? Here are a few possibilities:

- Use the debate to explore the idea of *ethics* – the name we give to the subject in which we reason about how we ought to live. Ask your group to identify the ethical elements in the debate about football.
- Invite them to list arguments for and against the view that professional football has been ruined by money.
- You might (surprisingly) find that the discussion moves into the realm of what philosophers, though probably not less academically motivated teenage students, call *teleology*: the

consideration of ends. What is the point of football? What is it for? Is it just a form of entertainment? Or does sport have some further purpose – perhaps even a moral purpose? And if so, how is that relevant to the way professional sport is funded? (In Chapter 4, we will explore how a worthwhile project could develop from such questions).

- Then – if time and attention has not already run out – you could start to explore the different ways in which ethical arguments are constructed. How do we decide what is the right thing to do? Ideas to explore here include: by appeal to rules, by thinking about consequences and by considering ideals such as fair play and sportsmanship.
- As a parting shot, you might suggest to the group that the question they have discussed would be a good starting point for a research project. As an extension, then, they should do some web research to find three relevant sources of information, only one of which is allowed to be a football fanzine.

Ethical frameworks

When exploring the questions of ethics, we do not all start from the same place. We operate with different ideas about what makes an action right or wrong. Philosophers have distinguished a number of 'ethical frameworks' which correspond to the main approaches which people bring to bear when they are asked to reason about what ought to be done. An initial division is between those who say that whether or not an action is right is a matter of its *consequences* and those who deny this. To be a consequentialist is to hold that the right thing to do is the action which brings about the best consequences for the greatest number of people. But what counts as a 'good' consequence? For traditional consequentialists, the key thing is happiness. According to classical utilitarianism, of the kind espoused by Jeremy Bentham and John Stuart Mill, the right thing to do is the action which promotes the greatest happiness for the greatest number of people.

The question of defining happiness is a problem here, as is the problem of 'adding up' happiness. What is happiness? Can we talk about 'quantities' of happiness? How would we measure it? How is it related to ideas such as pleasure, or well-being? Is a little happiness for many better or worse than great happiness for a few?

Problems such as these have led contemporary ethicists to re-examine the idea that some things are just right or wrong, regardless of the consequences. This is sometimes called an 'absolutist' approach. Traditionally, an absolutist approach to ethics has been associated with a 'divine command' theory of morality: the theory that the right thing to do is what God commands. In a secular age, when belief in God is less widespread and there is greater awareness of the plurality of ideas about what the divine will requires, philosophers have explored the possibility of providing an objective humanist foundation for ethics. The idea from which humanist accounts begin is that there are some things which are clearly conducive to human well-being, and other things which are clearly harmful. On this foundation, a framework of rights and duties can be constructed, which prescribes the obligations we have to others on account of their humanity. Once a rights and duties framework has been introduced for human beings, it seems natural to extend it to other sentient creatures – hence we get the idea of animal rights.

These different approaches to thinking about ethics – consequentialism, a framework of rights and duties, and an ethic based on religious teaching – can emerge naturally as part of ethical discussion in the classroom. Suppose a class is asked a question such as: 'Is it ever right to lie?' Some students will immediately turn to consequentialist considerations: What is at stake? Will a lie avoid needless suffering? Others will turn to the teaching of religion, perhaps citing the Ninth Commandment, 'Thou shalt not bear false witness.' And some students will think that we have a duty to tell the truth and that people have a right not to be misled. Students might also give reasons which fit within a framework of virtue ethics (one which is based on strengths of character). They might, for instance, appeal to the value associated with character traits such as honesty, as well as compassion.

Is it at all likely that we going to sort these debates out in the classroom? Will we reach consensus about the right thing to do, or the reasons which justify the right course of action? Probably not – but that is not really the point. The principal aim of these discussions is to help students appreciate that the way to deal with ethical problems is by a process of reasoning. A secondary aim is to bring to students' attention the fact that, when we do reason about ethics, we do so in quite different ways. Some people are moved by religious teaching, as it is integral to their sense of identity and a part of the life of the community to which they belong. Others are not. Some find consequentialist arguments compelling to the point of self-evidence. Others think that the idea that the end justifies the means is appalling. Some believe that a framework of rights and duties can provide a secure foundation for ethics. Others do not believe that it can. It is an inescapable fact that we approach ethics from very different standpoints.

The existence of plural approaches to ethical questions poses both an educational challenge – in that our task is to find a way to facilitate reasoned discussion in the face of fundamental disagreement – and also an opportunity, in that it is the fact of disagreement at this level which creates the impetus for students to begin to think seriously about their own views, how they can respond to those who differ, and how they must appear in the eyes of others.

In the light of this plurality, it is useful, when beginning the study of ethics, to teach students a little about some common ethical frameworks. In a post-16 programme, it would be appropriate to introduce the following:

- Consequentialism (or utilitarianism)
- The divine command theory
- A rights and duties framework
- Virtue ethics.

These frameworks can then be used as an analytical tool when different issues are being explored (see, for example, PoS Project Team, 2007a and 2007b and Swinbank and Taylor, 2009a and 2009b). The use of this approach does not imply that each framework is considered to be 'equally valid'. Frameworks are there to provide a tool for helping to give structure to ethical discussion, and provide students with some ethical vocabulary to use. Students will be able to begin identifying these frameworks when others use them. They can also be challenged to begin thinking about how they would describe their own ethical standpoint, and to think about the foundations of their own ethical thinking.

I tend not to introduce ethical frameworks in quite the same way with pre-16 students. Here, it is helpful to invite them to think about how people go about deciding what to do. Students will, with a little encouragement, usually identify 'consequences' or 'results' as being important: to see whether an action is good or bad, it is wise to think about what it leads to. Students might also mention the ideas of rights and religious teaching. I explain that these three – consequences (or, more memorably, results), rights and religious teaching – are all worth discussing when exploring an ethical question.

With able pre-16 students, or most post-16 students, some of the strengths and limitations of each framework can be explored. So, for instance, a class could be asked to think about the following questions:

- Is there anything which is so bad it ought never to be done, no matter how helpful the consequences might be? If so, what makes that action bad?
- Where do rights come from? Is it simply that we have laws which state that people have rights – or do rights rest on something more fundamental?
- Plato's Euthyphro dilemma can be posed. Is something good because God says so (in which case, killing an innocent child would be good, if God commanded it)? Or does God call things good because they are good (in which case goodness is independent of God's commandments)?

Ethical citizenship

Citizenship studies provide an excellent context within which to introduce students to the study of ethics. At the school where I teach, we overhauled our citizenship programme for 14–16-year-old students a number of years ago, making it, in effect, a programme in which students are introduced to some philosophical and ethical ideas, then invited to apply these in carrying out a research project addressing a socially pressing question.

The central idea behind the programme is that the ideal of a good citizen is an ethical one. A good citizen is someone who is well informed, ethically aware and able to engage in discussion and debate of the important questions facing society today. To prepare for this, then, it makes sense to give students an introduction to ethical reasoning, and provide them with an opportunity to develop their skills through a small-scale research project on a question with an ethical dimension to it. The following questions can be used for initial discussion, or as titles for project work:

- Should patients who wish to end their life be allowed help to die?
- Should Muslim students be allowed to wear traditional Islamic dress rather than school uniform?
- Should we use pig hearts for transplant into human patients (we already transplant pig valves into human hearts, I explain – so why not go the whole hog)?
- Is it wrong to use someone else's broadband connection without their knowledge?

A framework for philosophical discussion

Our emphasis is on learning through discussion. But we have seen that some didactic teaching, about commonly held beliefs, or core ethical frameworks, can help to stimulate and inform the discussion process. There is a place too for some didactic instruction about the character of philosophical argument. It helps if students understand the elements of dialectic.

In some critical thinking course, a lot of time is spent on this. Students are taught all about formal and informal logic, argument structure, common fallacies, and so forth. I don't think much of this is necessary – at least not at the outset. We should aim to hit the ground running and get straight into philosophical debate. Students learn to think by thinking. The analysis of what makes a piece of reasoning good or bad can come later. But it does help to say a little to students about the *type* of discussion which goes on in philosophy.

I use a very simple framework for philosophical discussion. It is short enough to be explained within a few minutes to a class, and it provides a useful tool for helping them to understand how philosophy works. It is a structure which they can apply in other contexts as well – when, for example, they are writing philosophical arguments of their own, and also when they are analysing arguments in other subject areas. The model is based on an approach developed by Sergia Hay in the context of teaching an online moral issues course (Hay, 2005). It looks like this:

- Point of view
- Argument
- Counter-argument
- Response

I explain to students that philosophy is a subject which examines the arguments people give for their beliefs about fundamental questions. The first thing to note is that the emphasis is firmly placed on argument. To enter the world of philosophy is to accept an invitation to an argument. In philosophy, it is not sufficient simply to assert beliefs: they need to be supported by a process of logical reasoning. Students need to appreciate that in philosophy, we use *reason,* not feelings, or appeals to authority, to support ideas. When asked to give a philosophical reason for a belief, it is not enough to say, 'It's what I would *like* to believe', or 'It is what my mother/father/teacher/favourite stand-up comedian believes.' What counts as a philosophical reason is an objective ground for believing that the view being put forward is likely to be true.

I then go on to explain that because philosophy is about the most fundamental questions of all, it is bound to be controversial. Different people answer the questions of philosophy in quite different ways. Philosophy is a conversation between these viewpoints. It involves continuous discussion and debate. Most of the time, philosophers argue. These arguments are not just quarrels, such as a child might have with his sister about who gets to play with the toy boat in the bath. The aim of philosophical argument is to determine where the truth lies. It involves evaluating how good the reasons someone gives really are.

As an illustration of this, students could be asked to consider a debate about the existence of God. Suppose a philosopher called Bill says that he believes in God. This is an expression of a point of view. If asked why he believes this, Bill might say that God must exist because the universe had to have a cause. This is an argument in favour of Bill's point of view. A second philosopher called Ben could evaluate this argument and decide that it was not valid. The fact that the universe has to have a cause is not a reason for believing in God, since there could be other causes. Perhaps the universe emerged from an earlier universe, Ben suggests. This is a counter-argument. Bill might respond by saying that we would still need to explain where the earlier universe came from (and Ben will, no doubt, have a counter-argument to Bill's response as well).

The structure of the philosophical exchange between Bill and Ben can be shown as follows:

- Point of view: God exists.
- Argument: The universe had to have a cause.
- Counter-argument: Perhaps the universe emerged from an earlier universe.
- Response: But you would still need to explain where the earlier universe came from.

The philosophical term to describe the process in which the statement of a point of view is followed by argument, counter-argument and response is 'dialectic'. An example such as the exchange between Bill and Ben can be helpful in explaining the dialectical character of philosophical discussion. There is a great deal more that could be said about the logical form of philosophical arguments. But the main purpose of the dialectical model is to provide a means by which students can start to analyse arguments, and to give them a framework to use when constructing arguments of their own. So it is best to proceed to these tasks, rather than spending time developing a more sophisticated account of the structure of argument.

Climbing the ladder of logic

When using the dialectical model to train students in the art of philosophical discussion, it is best to begin with activities in which they are asked to analyse other people's arguments. Once they have formed some grasp of the idea of argumentative structure, they can be asked to begin constructing arguments for themselves. Students tend to find it harder to create their own arguments than to identify arguments given by other people. The final stage – which is harder still – is to learn to identify and respond to counter-arguments against their own views. The questions, 'What argument would persuade me to change my mind? How would I respond to this argument?' are challenging ones. But as we noted at the start of this chapter, responsiveness to counter-argument is one of the hallmarks of rational enquiry.

To get to the point where students are beginning to think in this way, it is worth thinking about sequencing discussions to ensure that activities are in place to develop the more basic elements of philosophical reasoning, followed by the more challenging ones. The following sequence indicates one way this can be done:

1. Students are taught the distinction between a point of view and an argument. They practise identifying each of these elements in written arguments (from newspapers, blogs, magazines, video clips, etc.).
2. During discussions, students practise giving arguments to support their own philosophical views. Staging a classroom debate on an ethical or philosophical topic is one way to do this.
3. Students are taught that there are counter-arguments to philosophical propositions, and they practise identifying them. This can be done by selecting a well-written opinion piece from a newspaper, or a report of a court case, and asking students to list arguments and counter-arguments. Philosophical dialogues such as Hume's *Dialogues Concerning Natural Religion* are another good source. There are also many excellent videoed debates available on the internet about ethical issues or philosophical topics such as the existence of God. Students can be asked to watch an extract and analyse the structure of argument and counter-argument. A discussion thread following a web article can also be a good source, though you will need to select an extract where there is a reasonable quality of argument, rather than just emotive airing of opinion.
4. Students should learn to identify counter-arguments to their own viewpoint and practise responding to these. This can happen following a debate in the class, by asking students what they thought was the best argument against their own position, and how they would answer it.

These steps form a 'ladder of logic'. A carefully phased sequence of discussion activities can help students to progress to the higher rungs. Like any ladder, the ladder of logic can take you to various heights, depending on the height that the foot of the ladder is placed at and how far up you climb. Although the skills required to get to the higher rungs are more sophisticated than those at the base, there is nothing to stop a younger or a less able student from going to the top of the ladder. It is just that the ideas which they think about are likely to be less demanding. We might expect a pre-16 student to be able to identify and construct arguments and counter-arguments for a topic such as whether reality television shows are a good thing or not. They are less likely to engage productively with a discussion of the ethics of genetic screening, for example, where a grasp of the relevant philosophical arguments presupposes more advanced scientific knowledge.

Managing philosophical discussion

Here are some concluding pointers about the management of philosophical discussion:

- There is a fine line, in philosophical discussions, between intervening to direct the flow and allowing the conversation to find its own course. Try to assess the value of the conversation by the quality of reasoning which is going on. The trick is to intervene with nudges and prompts which can help to ensure that the discussion flows freely, but stays focused, and that a coherent line of argument and counter-argument can unfold.
- All philosophical discussions need close monitoring by the facilitator. Earlier in the discussion, you should be looking to see that a range of ideas is being expressed, so that there is plenty of material for students to pick up on and respond to.
- If the group is settling into an easy consensus, you may choose to play devil's advocate and challenge their assumptions, even if you agree with their position.
- Research has drawn attention to the valuable role of extreme views in philosophical discussion. You will want to encourage the expression of 'outlying' viewpoints. The best discussions are those in which clearly contrasting viewpoints are put forward. This is exactly the sort of stimulus which calls for students to begin thinking for themselves about which views they agree and disagree with.

- The overall direction of the discussion needs to be monitored. It may be necessary to remind the group of the main question under discussion, if, as often happens, the discussion wanders into other areas. Don't be afraid to put the brakes on a discussion which is drifting away from the main topic, even if it is going well. You could do this without being too heavy-handed by reminding students of a really perceptive remark that was made earlier, and which you think is worth further exploration.

- You should ask clarificatory questions as a matter of course. 'That was an interesting idea – can you explain what you meant by it?', 'Can I just ask us all to pause. We have been using a particular word and I wonder how we all understand it?' and so on.

- Philosophical discussions have a natural lifetime. If the discussion is beginning to wane, you will need to decide whether to intervene to inject new life, perhaps by introducing a new argument or saying something deliberately provocative. If you decide to play devil's advocate, you may need to choose your words carefully, as the group will be unimpressed if they decide you are being disingenuous. So you might preface your interjection with a qualifier such as, 'I'm not saying I believe this, but suppose I were to say the following . . . How would you respond?'

- You may want to draw a discussion to a close, then move on to provide some further stimulus material, and reopen the discussion with a new question on a related theme. A benefit of planning to use two or three short discussion activities is that you then have flexibility: if the first is running well, you can curtail the others. If the first discussion doesn't take off, you can move swiftly on.

- Varying the format of the discussions helps to keep students on their toes, and gives you a useful tool with which to contain any difficult or overly dominant members of the group. So one discussion might involve the whole group; the next might involve subgroups or pair-work. Or you could use 'snowballing', when students first discuss in pairs, pairs then join to make groups of four, and finally the whole class is brought together. You might insist that everyone contributes something, by going around the group one at a time. Or you might ask representatives from the subgroups to report back in a plenary session. Sometimes, if you have particularly able students with a confident presence, you can hand over the facilitatory role to them.

- Some students, after they have been part of a series of philosophical discussions, grow dissatisfied and say things like, 'But what is the point of these conversations? We never get any answers. What are we really learning?' Here, the ladder of logic can come to your aid. If you have planned the discussions carefully, so that each successive discussion requires students to take a step up to a higher rung, then you will be able to point out that the progress which the students have been making is progress towards better philosophical thinking skills. They may not be learning a great deal of new factual knowledge and they almost certainly won't be learning 'the answers' to the major philosophical questions. But they will be learning how to reason for themselves about these questions, and as a result, learning something about how to reason well about other sorts of question as well.
- Be quite firm about intellectual standards. It isn't a matter of 'anything goes'. Explain the importance of defending ideas using reason. Be ready, gently, to probe the student who thinks they can offer points of view with no argumentative support.
- Have confidence in philosophy. With the right sort of gentle prompting, students will open up. If your initial stimulus question is met by silence, it is quite probably a sign that minds are whirring. If the topic hasn't grabbed your students' interest or if it is incomprehensible to them, it won't be silence which follows but pointed remarks or the onset of displacement activities. So don't jump in nervously to fill the silence – but wait for students to begin framing thoughts of their own.

Table talk

We end this chapter with an extract from an online discussion between some students participating in the Philosophy Zone programme. The thread starter was the question: 'Is the table in front of you real?'

Posted by Helen

If a table was a figment of our imagination then it is unimaginable to think that our mind has created such a detailed and realistic object. If the table is a figment of our imagination then isn't it possible to imagine that our day to day lives are also a figment of our imagination? Is this possible?

Posted by Lauren

I disagree. The brain is more than capable of creating such a detailed image. For example, it is possible to imagine something you've seen quite clearly in your head and some people such as savants can create remarkable works of art without having to have the item in front of them.

Posted by Katie

Surely this ability of savants to create an elaborate piece of artwork without anything to copy from or guide them merely uses the imagination – which, whilst it is able to conjure up images in our mind, can't do so to the extent that your comment suggests. Furthermore, the fact that all five of our senses confirm the evidence that our eyes observe – we can taste, feel and smell things as well as see them – is evidence enough for the reality of the things we see.

Posted by Daisy

Each of our senses combine to give us the firm idea in our minds that the table is physically present, and as this is all we have to judge the world by, it is logical to presume, therefore, that it exists. However, if you think about it at the molecular level, only a small amount of the table does exist, as the actual size of the nuclei of the atoms that make it up is tiny, and the majority of it is just empty space deflecting light in a certain way. This is confusing to think about!

This discussion nicely exemplifies the elements from the model of philosophical discussion which we have been exploring. Helen opens the batting with an argument – a reductio ad absurdum – of the proposition that the table in front of you could exist merely in your imagination. She draws out an implication of this thought – namely that it entails that, potentially, everything in everyday life is merely imaginary – and she questions whether this is possible. (Helen's position could be backed up by an argument advanced by Gilbert Ryle, who argued that it makes no sense to suppose that one could be deceived about everything, because the concept of deception only gets its meaning by a contrast with situations involving true perception.)

Helen's argument is followed by a counter-argument from Lauren. She argues that there is a possibility that the table is a creation of the brain. She backs up her point of view by reference to the remarkable powers of imagination possessed by savants. Her argument is in turn countered by Katie, who questions the scope of the imagination, and also launches an argument based on the corroborative testimony of the different senses.

This first phase of the exchange exemplifies the argument/counter-argument structure. In the final post of the thread, Daisy agrees with Katie's argument for the reality of the table. But she can see a problem with this conclusion. Physics depicts a physical object as a field of tiny particles, each of which is surrounded by a large tract of empty space. This seems to suggest that the apparently solid table is an illusion.

Daisy has identified what Socrates called an 'aporia': a philosophical puzzle. We are torn between saying that the table is a solid, real physical object and saying that it isn't solid at all but is instead mostly empty space. The apparently clear concept of a solid physical object suddenly appears baffling. We thought that we knew what a table was, but, once we begin to think about it, we realize that we do not. The discussion has led to a moment of Socratic insight: it has led to the realization that we do not know what we thought we knew. It is from such moments that further, deeper philosophical enquiry begins.

3 Philosophy within the Curriculum: How to Develop a Project-Based Approach

Project-based philosophy

The dominance of written examinations in our current educational system tends to squeeze out space for thinking in general and reflective, philosophical enquiry in particular. We have considered how a programme of philosophical discussion with students has a lot to offer by way of exciting their interest in ideas, and equipping them to think better for themselves. In this chapter, we are going to explore how a student research project, on a philosophical theme, provides a natural next step. It is tremendous to have the exciting discussions, but students need to have an academic challenge to work towards if they are to gain the maximum benefit from their encounter with philosophy. For reasons that should by now be clear, a programme of philosophical study culminating in a written examination does not work well if what we want to do is develop a student's capacity for philosophical reflection. A student project, on the other hand, has great potential. It provides an ideal opportunity for deeper reflection, sustained thought, independent research and the development of a personal perspective.

Schools may prefer to run a programme of philosophical education as part of their curriculum enrichment programme, without using a formal qualification as an outcome. Good work can be done with students via an informal approach. So, for example, a school might decide to use some teaching time simply to hold philosophical discussions, and ask students to work on a personal philosophical project which will not be assessed. Given that much of the value of a philosophical approach to learning lies in the way that it *deepens* students, there is a case for doing work of this sort regardless of whether it leads to a qualification. Moreover, even if a grade is not given at the end, philosophical project work can be given recognition through what students choose to write on their personal statements when making university applications and through teacher references. Gaining a formally assessed qualification need not be the goal.

All that said, we cannot escape from the fact that students will take a task more seriously if it does lead to a qualification. If they are going to be asked to spend a significant portion of their time taking part in philosophical discussions and working on a philosophy project, they ought to have the opportunity to gain formal recognition for the work they have done. We turn, then, to a brief survey some of the qualifications which permit such an approach.

The Extended Project Qualification

The Extended Project Qualification is a pre-university qualification available in the United Kingdom and to international centres which offer A levels (the main qualification for post-16 students seeking to go on to academic courses at university). The Extended Project Qualification gives students an opportunity to carry out an extended research project on a question of their own choosing. An Extended Project Qualification is usually done over one or two years, alongside three to five other main subjects of study.

Although the emphasis is on students learning to work independently on projects, teaching is still necessary. Students need to be taught the skills and techniques that they will require when working on their projects. They also need an opportunity to discuss ideas as part of the important process of choosing the title for their project. Once project work is underway, students are expected to have regular meetings with a project supervisor, to review progress and discuss problems. Projects may take various forms, including a written dissertation, a scientific investigation or field study, a performance, or the creation of an artefact. Students often give oral presentations which are followed by questions from their assessor. Projects are assessed internally, with sampling and moderation of marks by teams of trained external examiners.

Since its launch in 2008, the Extended Project Qualification has grown rapidly in schools and colleges. One of the reasons why it is proving so attractive to schools and colleges is that it offers the opportunity for the development of a higher education model of learning within a secondary context. It is, therefore, of value as a preparation for the challenges of university study, a point made by the 1994 group of research-intensive UK universities:

> The Extended Project is widely welcomed in principle and in prospect. A large majority of departmental admissions tutors expect to recognise it as a positive attribute when selecting among applicants with similar levels of achievement (both high fliers and those at the borderline). Tutors also welcome its potential to enhance study skills, to align with under-graduate modes of study and to provide additional diagnostic evidence when selecting among applicants.
> (1994 Group, 2008, p. 6)

There is a natural connection between the Extended Project Qualification and the philosophical approach to education which we have been exploring. During project work, students should be questioning and thinking for themselves. They are expected to think more deeply, more independently and more critically. A programme of philosophical discussion, as we have seen, is an effective way of developing students' skills in these areas. It also provides students with the stimulus that they need to start 'thinking outside the box': to start asking questions which go beyond the syllabus. For these reasons, I advocate using an introduction to philosophy as part of the preparation students receive before they go on to work on their Extended Projects. An introduction to philosophy using the discursive, Socratic pedagogy described in Chapter 2 is an excellent way of preparing students for the challenge of independent project work.

Philosophical learning within the International Baccalaureate

Philosophy is integral to the International Baccalaureate (IB) Diploma programme. The IB Theory of Knowledge course is a compulsory part of the Diploma. It emphasizes an exploration of the philosophical dimension of knowledge and ways of knowing. Another compulsory component of the Diploma is the Extended Essay, a student research paper of up to 4,000 words in length. The Extended Essay is similar to the Extended Project Qualification in that both should extend a student's subject knowledge. However, this criterion is interpreted more strictly for the Extended Essay. For the Extended Project Qualification, it would be acceptable to explore ideas in a cross-curricular fashion; indeed, this is encouraged. With the Extended Essay, it is necessary to choose a subject area and then stay within those boundaries. So, for instance, it would not be acceptable to explore philosophical issues within a Physics Extended Essay. If IB students wish to explore a philosophical question, they should opt to write a Philosophy Extended Essay.

The Extended Essay requires students to engage in research to provide an evidence base for their writing. Students are expected to develop their own arguments. Writing should not be merely descriptive, but should involve analysis, synthesis and evaluation (IBO, 2011). As with the Extended Project, then, participation in philosophical discussion, where the emphasis is on analysing concepts, exploring links between ideas and learning to argue well, is a good way of preparing students for work on their Extended Essays.

Philosophy within the pre-16 curriculum

At what age should students begin to explore philosophy? There is a movement within the United Kingdom, and internationally, devoted to 'Philosophy for Children' (P4C). Children of primary school age who experience P4C sessions have an opportunity to begin discussing philosophical questions. The rationale here is that these questions often occur quite naturally to children, are enjoyable to discuss, and help to promote an attitude of thoughtful enquiry. Given the enthusiasm with which these sessions are received, it is natural to ask how this promising starting point can be built upon.

A project-based philosophy programme provides an obvious answer to this question. There is value in all students between the ages of 13 and 16 following a programme in which they learn a little about how to think philosophically and then have an opportunity to explore ideas through a personal project. A programme like this provides an excellent context for helping students to develop as independent learners, as well as giving them an opportunity to engage with important ethical and philosophical questions.

There is a good case for saying that a philosophical approach ought to be part of the education of all students at this age. It need not involve creating an entirely new programme of study, but can be dovetailed in with programmes which already exist. In the United Kingdom, the Level 2 Higher Tier Project is an example of a qualification which supports this sort of programme. Designed for students at GCSE Higher Tier level (i.e. able students aged 14–16), the qualification is based on a programme of initial teaching followed by a student project. Philosophical project work can also be done as part of a programme of PSHE (Personal, Social, Health and Economic Education), religious education or citizenship education. The IB middle years programme includes a student project, which emphasizes skills in planning, research and personal reflection. These programmes demonstrate that there are plenty of opportunities for developing a philosophical approach within the pre-16 curriculum.

Thinking more deeply

One of the valuable features of a project-based approach is that it gives students a chance to think more deeply. But what do we mean by 'deep' thought? We mean, in part, enquiring into fundamental questions. In any area of learning, we make assumptions. These are the starting points from which we build – the 'first principles'. To think more deeply is to ask questions about these first principles. Why do we accept them? What happens if we don't? How certain can we really be about the things which we normally take for granted? Ever since Socrates, who saw his life's work as pointing out to people that they thought that they knew things which in fact they did not know, philosophers have questioned the assumptions of those around them. The purpose of this critical questioning – the Socratic method – is not to turn people into sceptics, who believe nothing, but to stimulate them to begin thinking for themselves about what they believe.

During most lessons, teachers concentrate on the business of helping students to acquire knowledge, rather than critically questioning its foundations. Philosophical questions about what we can really know for sure can lead to exciting and profitable discussion, but the pressure of having to get through the syllabus can mean that there is limited time to explore them. A teacher might also worry that too much questioning of foundations will undermine the task of simply getting students to learn things.

But on the other hand, if we expect students to learn to think for themselves, rather than just absorbing information uncritically, surely we ought to be encouraging them to explore these deeper questions? If we declare that critical questioning is off-limits, we close off the very path which students need to go down if they are to develop into independent thinkers. What we need is a context for the Socratic discussion to continue, when it goes beyond what can be done within a conventional classroom setting. Philosophical project work provides just such an opportunity. It gives students a chance to ask fundamental questions, and to think deeply and critically about the foundations of what they are learning. When Socratic enquiry begins in the classroom, project work provides a place for it to continue.

Consider, for example, a history lesson in which the question under discussion is: 'What was the cause of the First World War?' This is a question which makes certain philosophical presuppositions. It assumes, for a start, that historical events have causes. Since it refers to 'the' cause, it also presupposes that there was a single cause. A further tacit assumption of the lesson is that we can find out an answer.

Each of these assumptions can be questioned. Is it true that all events have causes? We tend to assume this, but is there any reason to do so? Why couldn't there be events which happen purely at random? And what makes us think that there is a single cause for an event? Couldn't there be multiple causes? And can we ever know for certain that what we think caused an event really did so? Is there any way to test claims about historical causes?

These are excellent questions to think about. They are questions which invite a student to think more deeply: to think, not just about the causes of a particular event, but about the nature of history and the limits of historical knowledge. They require a student to take a philosophical approach. They would thus provide good starting points for further research as part of a philosophical project.

Philosophical geography

Good philosophical project work can be done by inviting students to think about the philosophical dimension of what they are learning in their other subjects of study. Consider a Geography student who is writing an Extended Project about the perception of the risk of earthquakes among people living close to a geological fault-line. As part of the project, she studies the relevant secondary literature. She has a friend who lives in the San Francisco Bay area, and with her help, she carries out an online questionnaire survey of some of the inhabitants of the area. Her supervisor is keen, though, that she extends herself beyond the purely geographical aspects of the project. The project is about how people perceive risk – and this raises the wider, philosophical problem of perception. How do we perceive things? How is perception affected by our beliefs? Can two people look at the same thing and perceive it differently? Her supervisor points her towards the work of Thomas Kuhn – a philosopher who wrote about the way in which perception is affected by the beliefs we hold. She incorporates a discussion of this philosophical dimension of the question into her project.

Putting project-based programmes on the timetable

'Independent learning' is sometimes interpreted to mean that students should be assigned a task, then left to get on with it by themselves, mostly in their own time. A teacher might, for example, ask a class to work on an independent research project as a way of keeping them out of mischief during the long summer vacation. But I take the view that project work should be done during timetabled lesson time, as well as in the student's own time. I also think that students need to be taught how to do it properly. The value of project-based programmes as vehicles for helping students develop skills in critical thinking, independent research, extended writing and time management means that they deserve to be on the timetable every bit as much as more conventional subjects.

There is a slight air of paradox about the idea of *teaching* students to learn independently. Independent learning is the end product of a process which begins with training in the techniques of research, analysis, and the development, defence and presentation of arguments. Although students grow in independence, facilitation is needed at all stages of this process. This is self-evident, if we compare teenage students, beginning to think for the first time about philosophical questions, with the average undergraduate, or even post-graduate, who, with the advantage of several years more maturity, still requires considerable guidance and supervision. There are different interpretations of independent learning, but my own view is that you can't expect teenage students to do it without teaching them how.

When I describe this model to deputy heads or curriculum managers, I sometimes hear the sound of breath being sucked in. 'That is expensive', is what the more candid of them say. But to achieve the outcome of transforming the way in which students learn, an investment of resources is essential. The value of this approach lies in the results. I cannot myself see any better route to enhancing the capacity of students for independent learning. If we really value that outcome, we ought to be prepared to invest the resources.

Designing a project-based philosophy programme

A project philosophy programme is composed of two elements (see Table 3.1).

The first element in the programme is the taught course, the aim of which is to prepare students for philosophical project work. During the second part of the programme, students work on producing their philosophical dissertations, under the guidance of a supervisor. The production phase is structured in a way which corresponds to the different sections of the dissertation, which we will examine in Chapter 4.

When thinking about what to teach during the taught course part of the programme, it is important to remember that the main aim is to get students ready to choose, and start work on, their own project. It will not do to overload the programme of study with the teacher's favourite ideas. Nor will it do to make students learn a great deal of information about the history of ideas from the Greeks to the present day (the 'Plato to Nato' approach). The point of the taught course is to equip students with the skills to begin fashioning and defending their own ideas. Here, a case-study approach can work well. The best case studies are ones which are interesting and controversial, so that they naturally lead to debate. Case studies should also inspire ideas for possible projects.

Table 3.1 A project-based philosophy programme

Taught Course	Research skills
	Philosophical frameworks and thinking skills development
	Ethical enquiry
	Case-study exploration to stimulate ideas for projects
Production of Philosophical Dissertation	Project planning
	Researching documentary sources
	Drafting literature review
	Drafting discussion section
	Top and tailing
	Editing dissertation
	Evaluation of project

Table 3.2 Ideas for case studies

Science and religion	The idea of beauty
Nature and nurture	The idea of goodness
Free will and fate	The ideal society
Truth and myth	Justice
Changing attitudes towards the natural world	The self
Humanity's treatment of other species	The limits of knowledge
The supernatural	Warfare
Mind, body and soul	Health and well-being

These broad topic areas can be used as starting points for research exercises, philosophical discussion and classroom debate. They can be studied using a cross-curricular approach. They also provide an indication of themes which can be explored within the context of a philosophical dissertation. However, as each case study covers a broad range of issues, as they stand they would not make particularly suitable dissertation titles. A dissertation should focus on a single issue. Students should, therefore, be encouraged to look for a specific research question which falls within an area of interest to them.

Case studies can also be chosen to overlap with students' other areas of study, so that they can bring their existing subject knowledge into the discussion (see Table 3.2).

Key features of a project philosophy programme

- Teaching happens chiefly through Socratic mentoring.
- Learning happens chiefly through philosophical discussion.
- The programme includes a small amount of didactic teaching about research methods, techniques for philosophical argument and project management skills.
- Teaching is organized around case studies. These are selected for (a) student and teacher interest (b) suitability for skills development and (c) potential for further exploration in a research project.
- Research skills are developed using short assignments before project work begins.
- Core philosophical and ethical frameworks are introduced.
- The programme is not examined but forms the basis for philosophical project work.
- The study materials should provide an opportunity for students to develop their skills in research, analysis and critical reasoning.

Is Socrates in the staff room?

If you are a school leader, turning your thoughts towards the question of the cultivation of a philosophical ethos within your school, the question of which teachers can teach in this way will be at the forefront of your mind. At the moment, many schools employ teachers who have some knowledge of philosophy, perhaps because it formed a component of their degree course, or perhaps because they are already teaching elements of it, as part of religious education, say. It is still comparatively rare for a school to employ a full-time professional philosophy teacher. But it should by now be clear that the approach to philosophically enriched education which I am advocating is a broad one, and thus, it does not have to be taught solely by a specialist philosopher. The principal requirement is that teachers understand what it means to adopt a reflective, philosophical perspective towards their teaching.

A good model is to share the teaching out among a cross-curricular team of staff, with some coordination from a 'chief Socratic mentor'. Students can then be taught to explore philosophical questions which arise within different subjects and at the boundaries between subjects. Organizing things in this way sends a message to students about the value and importance of thinking outside curriculum boxes.

Teachers who have themselves had to go through the mill of writing research projects tend to have a more intuitive, and sympathetic, understanding of the particular challenges which students doing similar project work will face. So if you have, among your staff, a teacher with a research degree or a qualification which involved extensive research project work, such a person will be a good one to involve in setting up your project programme.

It may well be that such a teacher will already be known to you for their love of argument, as well as their love of ideas – a love which means that they find it hard to confine themselves within their own discipline. Socratic mentors may well be involved in teaching citizenship, critical thinking, general studies or religious education, and they will jump at the chance to help spread philosophical thinking throughout the curriculum.

> **A job description for a Socratic mentor**
>
> - Loves argument
> - Strong academic pedigree but willing to help the less able climb the ladder of logic
> - Comfortable being the 'guide at the side' not the 'sage on the stage'
> - Generally interested in most topic areas
> - Knows their way around a research project (ideally, because they have a degree with a research component)

Research skills

A capacity for research is needed for any philosophical enquiry. Students need to be able, when asked a question, to go and find for themselves some relevant source materials, and know how to make use of their sources in addressing the question. In a programme designed to lead up to work on an individual student project, this is a foundational skill. Whatever type of project students choose to work on, research will be required.

This means that there has to be a transfer of responsibility, so that instead of expecting the teacher to provide all the answers, students begin to enquire for themselves. Students are accustomed to being given information in easy-to-digest form. They have at their disposal the enormous (and enormously variable) resource of the internet – so that, when asked to carry out some research for themselves, it seems straight-forward enough to them: type in their question to a good search engine, and print out the answer from the website at the top of the list. Many are genuinely surprised to find that this isn't quite what is required. They will need to understand the different activities which form the research process. I would identify the following as important steps in research:

- Collection: Gathering up sources of information
- Selection: Choosing the most relevant sources
- Analysis: Asking questions about the meaning of the source material
- Synthesis: Linking sources into a coherent narrative
- Evaluation: Assessing the reliability and validity of sources.

Ground-floor research: Collection and selection

Research begins with gathering up sources of information. Here, depending on the level of ability and age of the students you are working with, you may want to be more or less demanding. With a low ability pre-16 group, you may want to make things as simple as possible by providing the sources of information yourself – bring a pile of books or articles and spread them out in the classroom – and ask students to start selecting from these. With post-16 students, you might want to set a short research exercise, in which students are expected to find for themselves two or three sources of different kinds (i.e. not just websites) which are relevant to a specified question. It is at this stage that you may want to explore with students the range of source types which are available to them – books, magazines, journal articles, as well as a vast range of higher quality academic material which can be accessed freely online. The value of signing on at a local library might need to be explained, and they may need guidance in accessing source material via online archives.

Once they have collected some sources, students will need help in understanding how to extract relevant material from them. It is important not to take for granted things which will seem obvious to those of us who grew up with books as our primary source of information, rather than the internet. Many students wilt at the sight of a hefty book, since they imagine that they will have to read it from cover to cover. It helps to explain some techniques for skim reading:

- Chapter headings and subheadings are there for a reason. Students can use these to help locate where they should start reading.
- In well-written prose, the opening sentence in a paragraph usually provides an indication of what will be discussed in it. A student can skim through an article or chapter by reading the first sentence of each paragraph, until they find the most useful section to begin reading more closely.
- It often does not occur to students that the index at the back of a book might actually be helpful in locating the information they

need. I have seen eyes light up when I have taken a book from a student, opened it at the back, and pointed to the entry in the index corresponding to the topic they are researching.

I should make clear that I do not think of skimming as an alternative to close reading. It is simply a technique which helps students past the obstacle that confronts them when they realize that they will have to work their way through a lot of material before they find what they need. Students working on extended research projects often find the scale of the project daunting. In the early stages, they gaze at the destination and think they will never get there. The trick is to make taking the next step look possible. For students doing research for the first time, this means helping them to get to the point at which they are beginning to discover useful material for themselves.

The other stumbling block for students at the selection stage is that of keeping track of the source materials they have looked at. It is a general rule that students – like all of us – will naturally prefer the line of least resistance, which is to spend time allocated to research in simply reading. This is because reading is less hard work than reading and writing. I have seen students occupy themselves, apparently productively, for a period of months, in reading about their chosen topic, with scarcely a note to show for all the time they have spent. Without some record of what has been read, it is going to be very difficult for such students to write anything up.

At an early stage in their training in research methods, students should be taught about the conventions for academic citation and referencing. Here again, the temptation to leave this to the end is strong – but again, it is going to be difficult for students to reconstruct the research trail if they haven't been keeping records as they go. Here, a well kept reading log can be very valuable.

It is also important to address the issue of plagiarism early on. Students do not necessarily appreciate that information which they have found cannot simply be included in their own work without citation. Prevention is much better than cure, and one of the merits of addressing protocols for including quotations and using citations at an early stage is that you cut down the risk that students will use unattributed material, intentionally or not, in their own project.

Some students – typically lower ability pre-16 students – do not ever get further than ground-floor research. For these students, research is mainly about collecting up source material, then selecting what is relevant for their own project work. For stronger students, however, the aim is not simply to collect and select, but to analyse and synthesize source material. These activities constitute higher-level research skills.

Higher-level research: Analysis and synthesis

For students who are able to do more than simply collect and select from source materials, their project should contain a well-constructed review of the research literature which relates to their chosen research question. What they should not do is simply write a paragraph on each source that they have read. Instead, they should *analyse* the information they have gathered. That is to say, they should think about what it means, and how it relates to their chosen question. They should explore connections between the different elements of their research: this is part of what we mean by *synthesis*. I explain to students that they should aim to write their review of the research literature as a narrative in which they address the main developments which underpin their project. They may choose to organize their literature review chronologically, so that it details the major developments in the area they are researching up until the present day. Alternatively, it may work better if they address a series of themes. In either case, what matters is that they are not simply stating what their sources have told them, but seeking to provide a coherent narrative, or set of narratives, of the developments and ideas which relate to their question.

Wikipediatrics

A vital element in the research process is that of the evaluation of research sources. Which of the sources that a student investigates can be regarded as reliable? How is it possible to distinguish between fact and opinion? Is the presentation of information in a documentary source biased or objective? These are easy questions to ask, but it is not at all easy for students to answer them. I have coined the term 'wikipediatrics' for the technique of assisting them in this vital task.

There is an entire branch of philosophy – epistemology – devoted to the question of how knowledge is possible. The sceptical challenge to knowledge arises because it is always possible that a claim may appear to be well supported by evidence, yet still not be true. Philosophers continue to discuss how serious a problem this is. Does it show, for example, that we are mistaken when we claim to know things? Or does it show that knowledge is possible, but that absolute certainty is not? However, this debate is viewed, the fact that appearances can be deceptive should lead us to proceed cautiously, and do what we can to check the reliability of our sources. In the case of students taking their first steps as researchers, it is helpful to encourage them to seek to corroborate sources (particularly websites) and to consider the provenance of source materials. It is usually possible to find answers to questions such as 'Who published this?', 'Has it been peer-reviewed?' and 'Is it a neutral piece of research or is the author biased in some way?' The answers to these questions should make a difference to the degree of confidence with which the source is used. If these questions *can't* be answered, then that fact is also significant, and should affect the extent to which the source is relied on. It is worth explaining to students that there is nothing wrong with using a source which is biased in some way, provided that allowance is made for this in the way it is used. So, for example, a table of data about animal research published by an anti-vivisection society may well represent the facts in a biased way. This is not a reason for discounting the source, however. Instead, it means that a student would need to make a careful evaluation of the quality of information. They should compare the presentation of data with other sources and, in the light of this cross-checking, draw conclusions about the way in which data has been interpreted.

I ask students to write brief evaluations of each source that they use, as evidence that they have considered these matters. But the most important thing is that the students learn to discriminate between sources of better and worse academic quality when they are at the collection and selection stage. Here, there is a need for the research supervisor to provide guidance. Unless the student is already familiar with the field, they will simply not be able to make judgements about the authority of different sources. So it is appropriate for the supervisor to guide the student towards places where good quality material is to be found.

Activities for developing research skills

- Give students a pile of recent newspapers. Ask them to select an interesting article and summarize key points from it.
- Ask students to keep a reading log, in which they keep notes on whatever they choose to read for a period of 2 or 3 days.
- Select an event and give the students 3 different news reports of this event. Ask them to evaluate each source in terms of reliability and bias. Ask them to consider what factual claims are made in each report, and how they could check these.
- Set students a mini-project assignment on a given topic (such as 'Time', 'God', 'The Mind', 'Language', etc). They should choose a research question which falls within this topic area (e.g. 'How have ways of measuring time changed?', 'What have different cultures believed about God?', 'How does language affect the way we think?', 'What is the unconscious?'). They should then find 3 research sources and write up a short (1,000 word) review of these sources. They should include proper source citations and a bibliography, and brief evaluations of each source.

Project Management: How to Supervise the Writing of Philosophy Dissertations

Chapter Outline

Project management

Writing a philosophy project is an exciting but challenging task for students. It offers them a chance to develop ideas and arguments in some depth. Managing students during the process of working on a dissertation is also exciting and challenging. Students need close supervision if they are to negotiate the hurdles that they will face. In this chapter, we will explore some general points about good practice in the management of student project work, as well as considering points which are relevant to philosophical dissertations in particular.

Choosing a research question

When students are making a start on their project, it is obviously important that they make a suitable choice of research question. The best questions are those for which there is relevant research material and which are 'open': that is to say, a variety of answers are possible, so that the student needs to engage critically, evaluating the merits of different responses.

I always encourage teachers to negotiate this all-important phase of the project with their students and not to rush the process of decision making. Choosing a question which lacks depth, or openness, or which is purely speculative, will mean that they will struggle when it comes to building a reasoned, argumentative response, in which they seek to bring research evidence to bear in support of their answer. There needs to be something to argue about and materials with which to build the arguments. It makes sense, then, to do some initial brainstorming, then send students away to do some research to see if they can lay their hands on useful source materials. If they can – that is a sign that they could be onto a good question. If they can't – it might be time to think again. In most projects, there is an interplay between thought about the research question, and the early phase of research. The student phrases a question, does some research, then modifies the question in the light of what they have found out. The fact that this process of refining the question is happening is usually a very healthy sign. Students are also relieved if they are told that you are not expecting their question to settle down straight away, and that it is a good thing if the question is refined as a result of research (though dramatic shifts midway through the programme are not to be encouraged).

Helping students choose a suitable research question

There are a number of criteria to emphasize to students when they are selecting a research question:

Is the question personally interesting?

A project can take a long time to complete, and the student will be more likely to get there if they choose a question which they find really interesting.

Is the question clear and well-focused?

Good projects usually develop in response to a clear, well-focused, specific research question. If the student decides simply to research a broad topic (e.g. 'The Dog'), their work is likely to lack focus, depth and direction.

Is the question one which can be researched?

All projects involve research, and it will be difficult for the student to make progress if there isn't much research material on their question (or if the only available materials are too complicated).

Is the question one which can be argued about?

A project is an opportunity for the student to put forward their own perspective. It will involve argument and debate between opposing viewpoints. So the question should be one which invites an argumentative response. If students are struggling to know what to write about, a good piece of advice is to suggest that they do some research to find out what questions in their subject area of interest are currently being debated. Their project can then be their own contribution to that debate.

A case study of the development of a good research question

A student is thinking about what to do for her philosophy project. She grows interested in the question of how children who commit serious offences, such as murder, are treated in the criminal justice system. Are we treating such children humanely? She discusses her question with her supervisor. They agree that it looks like a promising basis for a project. The issue is one that the student finds interesting. The question as it stands is quite clear. It

⇨

suggests a number of avenues for research: the pre-trial, trial and post-trial phases can each be examined. It is also a controversial question. On the one hand, we have the fact that terrible things have been done. On the other, we have the fact that children cannot be treated just as if they were adults. Working out how to assess the strength of arguments for and against proves to be a fascinating task. The student discovers that there are interesting international comparisons to be made. She researches child psychology, seeking to see if it can provide a clear basis for setting an 'age of criminal responsibility'. She also explores some of the philosophical issues surrounding the justification for punishment.

Using philosophy to open a closed question

Philosophy has a role to play in helping students to frame good questions for their projects. As a rule, in projects where students are expected to develop arguments of their own, it is better to choose open rather than closed questions. Questions with short, easily established factual answers are not going to lead to sustainable research projects. Once the answer has been found, the project will come to an abrupt end. Conversely, questions which cannot swiftly be answered by appeal to facts require the application of skills such as assessing evidence, evaluating the strength of argument and counter-argument and thinking creatively about what can be said when no clear-cut answer presents itself. If students are encouraged to choose a question with a philosophical dimension, they are more likely to come up with an open question, which in turn means that their project is more likely to contain interesting discussion of arguments.

So, for instance, a student who asks a question such as 'What qualifications do I need to become a physiotherapist?' is not well placed for a successful project. The question is a closed one: the answer can be found out with the assistance of a search engine in a matter of minutes. But suppose, now, that the student does some initial research and discovers that physiotherapy training used to be hospital-based but that now, physios take degree courses in universities. How, the student wonders, has this change in training affected the profession? She chooses to compare the merits of degree course and hospital-based training routes. What was a closed question is suddenly open. Now, there is scope for analysis and evaluation; there is something to argue about, and evidence to collect in favour of one or other option.

This is an example of how a closed question can be opened up. But the journey can go a stage further with some input from philosophy. Suppose now that the student asks some philosophical questions. What is physiotherapy? How is it different from other sorts of massage therapy? Is it a scientific pursuit, like medicine? Is it 'mainstream' or 'complementary' therapy, and how can we tell? What does it mean to be a good physiotherapist? What are the character traits – the virtues – which constitute excellence in the profession? These are philosophical questions – they are questions about what it is to be a physiotherapist; what the concept of physiotherapy really means. And clearly, these are questions which have been answered in different ways by different people.

We have moved from a closed question to an open one and then discovered that there is a philosophical dimension to be explored. This is a trajectory which takes a project away from simple collection and selection of facts, into analysis, synthesis and evaluation – and, ultimately, to a place where there is the potential for the student to begin to articulate and defend her own ideas, based on the findings of her research, about how she sees the profession she is aiming to enter, and what conclusions she has drawn about the way in which professional training has developed.

I do not think it is fanciful to expect students to think about questions like these. They will, of course, need support in order to learn how to frame such questions, and direction in order to know where to look to begin finding possible answers. They will need to be practised in the art of weighing up argument and counter-argument. With this sort of preparation, students can begin to address some quite deep, fundamental questions. Philosophical questions call for creative, reflective, analytical thought, which is why questions with a philosophical aspect have the potential to lead to rich, interesting projects.

Reason and emotion

Philosophy is connected to the search for meaning in life, and as such it has a significance which goes beyond simply assessing the logic of arguments for or against a proposition. Project work too has a part to play, and, at its deepest and richest, the journey a student goes on when they engage in research on a personally chosen question can be a journey of self-discovery. I emphasize to students that their choice of project should be underpinned by a personal rationale. They are going to spend a period of weeks, or possibly months, working on it. So it should be a question which is worth exploration. The issue they explore should be a significant one – both for them, and also, perhaps, for society at large.

Often, students choose their project based on their aspirations for future work or study. They may have made up their mind about what degree course they would like to study, and the project can be a means of demonstrating their interest in, and furthering their knowledge of, their chosen subject. Or it might be that they are aiming at a particular profession, and the project can be a part of their vocational preparation. I have seen excellent art, music and performance projects produced by talented young people who hope to go on to start their professional lives in the worlds of the visual and performing arts.

Sometimes, however, the project has a particular personal resonance. Family circumstances or medical problems – the daily realities with which students have to grapple – can sometimes become the stimulus for a journey of academic reflection. In this way, project work offers a space for the integration of reason and emotion. From difficult or painful experiences, a reflective journey, which involves exploration of how the problem has been examined through research and academic enquiry, can lead towards a fuller understanding. I have seen work from students addressing questions about the mental illness of a friend or family member, about gender and sexuality, about faith and doubt, and about a personal struggle with the management of a behavioural disorder. It is always moving to read the reports written by students who have taken this path. At their best, such projects exhibit a balance between the subjective feelings that motivated the project and the objective perspective that can be achieved through a careful, scholarly study of the question. These projects are all about the search for harmony between reason and emotion.

Philosophy for football fans

If you type the phrase 'philosophers football match' into Google, you will find that the classic Monty Python sketch from 1972 is still inspiring people to draw humorous connections between two seemingly disparate activities (see also Figure 4.1).

The Monty Python joke works because of the absurdity of the event. What could be more incongruous than philosophers on a football pitch? Yet it is not quite so incongruous for philosophers to *think* about football. Philosophical questions can arise from more or less any topic. In Chapter 2, I made the suggestion that a less academically motivated group of boys might enter the domain of philosophical argument as a result of their interest in football. Taking this a step further, could this lead into a full-blown project?

I think it could. Football, as a potential project topic, has the singular advantage that it interests boys. If you are going to get the average teenage boy to write a few thousand words, and stick with a single topic for several months of work, you had better be sure that the topic is one which

Figure 4.1 The philosophers' football match: Greece versus France

he finds interesting. This is an application of a point made by John Locke. Here is what he had to say about the foundations of good education:

> The great skill of a teacher is to get and keep the attention of his scholar: whilst he has that, he is sure to advance as fast as the learner's abilities will carry him; and without that, all his bustle and pother will be to little or no purpose. To attain this, he should make the child comprehend (as much as may be) the usefulness of what he teaches him; and let him see, by what he has learned, that he can do something which he could not do before, something which gives him some power and real advantage over others who are ignorant of it. (Locke, 1922, p. 132)

Two elements are significant here. The first is the importance of *getting the attention* of students and the second, the importance of showing students that what they are learning is actually of some use to them. Football is as good a way as any of getting and keeping the attention of a typical teenage boy. But we might wonder whether there is much educational utility to be had here. Once we have his attention, can we propel him gently along the pathway that leads to academic enquiry?

The key step is helping him to select an appropriate research question: one which combines a factual and a philosophical element. Or, to put it in terms I would use when explaining it to the teenage student, there needs to be something to find out – something to research – and something to argue about.

Football continues to score well on both counts. Most boys know where to go to find out data about the performance of their favourite team. They also know where to go to find arguments. The blogs are full of debate about, for instance, what the manager should have done with his players to prevent the dismal performance in the Cup final . . .

So we have some facts and we have some arguments. It would be stretching it, though, to say that we had entered philosophical territory. What is needed is *analysis* – not of scores, or tactics, but of ideas. Which ideas? Well, one would be the idea of football itself. It is a game played by competitive sportsmen. But which element is more important? Is it competition or sportsmanship? If what we really want in our sport is high quality competition, then we won't necessarily mind that the sport has become a profession in which vast salaries go to a small number of very talented players, and in which every inch of the team strip is covered with advertising, and that adverts even intrude onto the pitch. But if we think that sport is important because of particular ideals – team spirit, fair play and achievement for its own sake – then we are going to feel pretty uncomfortable about the excessively commercial character of elements of the modern game. Here, then, is something worth researching and arguing about. What is football for? A philosophical enquiry into the question of the purpose of football is a worthwhile project for a student who loves the game. Given their passion, there is a good chance that they will engage seriously with this enquiry.

In my experience, you can take a student into some really interesting philosophical territory, provided you are careful to start where they are, and show them the value of what they are being asked to learn – the second of Locke's points about good teaching. I am not pretending that a teenager's project on whether footballers are being too highly paid is likely to set the academic world alight. But I do know that if we start students in the right place, and lead them gently in the right direction, then they can be helped to do things of academic value, namely, learn a little about the need to back up opinions with facts, recognize that there is more than one side to many questions and begin to appreciate that behind many disputes lie some deeper questions, about what things mean and why they matter.

You might think that this approach lacks academic integrity and that we should be making students write their examination essays on questions we have chosen. But you will find that you simply won't get that far – at least, not very far with the all-important task of prompting students to ask questions and think for themselves. But for those who think that there is nothing as rigorous as an examination, please note that I am not suggesting that this is *all* we should do, just that it is an approach which works, does something useful, and can open some new doors.

Structuring philosophical dissertations

The sheer size of a major project can scare students off. At several thousand words in length, an Extended Project or Extended Essay could well be the single biggest piece of work the student has ever done. This creates a psychological barrier. Many students find it hard to imagine writing something of this size. I therefore introduce students to a framework for an academic dissertation (see Table 4.1). I explain to students that their project will be broken down into sections and that they will work on a section at a time. I also give them an indication of the length that the sections should be, the order in which they should work on them, and the style of writing which is appropriate to each.

In saying this, I could be accused of being too prescriptive about what is, after all, a piece of independent project work. Shouldn't the choice of structure be left up to the student? But this is a little like asking people who have never cooked to write a recipe book. Students will not know, before they begin, what is involved in writing a literature review, producing an analytical discussion, or writing an abstract. When we provide the structure, we are giving them a framework within which they can express their creativity. The structure is there to facilitate independent thought; it is not meant to be a strait-jacket.

It can help the teacher, too, if the dissertations produced by their students have the same structure. If you are supervising a large group, it

Table 4.1 A framework for a philosophical dissertation

Section	Contents
Title page	A statement of the research question
Table of contents	Headings of main sections Page numbers
Abstract	Brief overview of the entire dissertation
Introduction	An exploration of the research question Context for the project
Literature review	A thematic or chronological review of sources Citations for sources Evaluation of source reliability
Discussion	A clear statement of the philosophical point of view to be defended Arguments Counter-arguments Response to counter-arguments
Conclusion	Summary of argument
Evaluation	Reflections on the research process
Bibliography	List of references giving full details of sources used

is in your interest to keep students marching more or less in step. It will be much easier to keep track of what they are doing if they are all working on a particular section of the project at the same time. Having a prescribed structure for the finished project means that you can put in place a series of deadlines for each section (both at first draft and final hand-in stage). This can be sanity-preserving for the teacher, who otherwise will be trying to keep tabs on an entire group, each member of which is doing their own thing. (See Table 3.1 for an outline of the production stages of a philosophical dissertation).

Another benefit of a structured approach is that you can drip-feed guidance to students about the order of the project, what should be included in each section, and how different elements should be written. If left to themselves, they will assume that the first thing to write is the introduction. You will need to explain that this has to wait, since it is meant to reflect the entire project, and until the project has been drafted, it won't be clear what it is all about. They will not know how much time to spend on each section or how much to write. Again, by having a framework with recommended (though not mandatory) sectional word counts, you can help them produce a project with an appropriate balance between the sections. As their project will mainly involve researching a question, then producing their own arguments, they will spend most of their time working on the literature review and discussion sections. These should constitute the bulk of the project.

Supervising the writing of the literature review

Once they have framed a suitable research question, it makes sense for students to start the research process by writing a review of the relevant literature. This process will yield a body of opinion, ideas, information and historical fact from which the student can then proceed to construct arguments of their own. As the name suggests, the literature review is all about reviewing what other people have done or said. It is, therefore, a relatively accessible starting point for students who may well not yet know what they think about the question they have chosen to research.

It means too that when they do come to the stage of discussing argument and counter-argument, they should be well informed, both about what the main lines of argument are and about the context within which the argument takes place.

The following points about literature reviews are applicable to both pre-16 and post-16 students. The points marked (*) are mainly relevant to projects being produced by post-16 students.

References, citations and bibliographies

Every time a student uses a source, they should include a citation and a full reference in the bibliography. The reference should give enough information for someone else to find exactly what they have looked at. There is a variety of conventions for references and citations. The following is a clear and reasonably simple method:

- For a book or journal article, a reference should include the author's name, the full title of the book or article (and the journal title if relevant), the location and date of publication, the publisher and the page number.
- For a website, a reference should include the author (if this information is available), the title of the article, the title of the website, the date of publication (if known), the date of access and the full URL. If students cannot find the author's name they should use the name of the organization which hosts the webpage instead.
- Citations should use the name of the author, the date of publication, and the page number (e.g. Hawking, 2010, p. 10).
- The student should include a citation whenever they have used a source, whether they have quoted from it or simply used it for information.
- Students must keep track of sources as they go. It is almost impossible to recover this information at the end of the project.
- The list of references in the student's bibliography should include all the sources that are cited, but not sources they have read and not used.
- Some word processors can make life much easier for the student by keeping a record of sources, creating citations and automatically building the bibliography. It is worth drawing students' attention to this feature.

- Further guidance on referencing can easily be found by typing 'Harvard Referencing' into a search engine.

Source evaluation

The first time a source is used, I encourage students to write a short commentary in which they evaluate the quality of the source. This can be included as a footnote in the dissertation. Students can ask the following evaluative questions:

- What sort of information is the source providing?
- Is it reliable?
- Can information be corroborated by cross-checking against other sources?
- Is the source an acknowledged authority?
- Is source bias an issue?

The student's evaluative remarks should be genuine. Comments such as: 'It is Wikipedia, it is unreliable', or 'It is a national newspaper, it is reliable' are not particularly helpful. If students can't be sure of the quality of a source, they should ask whether to use it at all. If they decide to, they should be cautious about the use to which it is put.

Academic honesty

Students should not cut and paste material from the internet or lift material word for word from other sources. They need to understand that this counts as plagiarism and is unacceptable. I explain to students that research involves reading, selecting information, then expressing it in your own words. They may of course quote a source. But it is not acceptable to use material which comes straight from someone else's work without citation. If they have a good reason for quoting the exact words from a source (perhaps because it uses a particularly vivid phrase or 'soundbite' or because they want to quote something said by an expert) then they should use quotation marks (or some other clear way of distinguishing the quoted words from their own) and give a reference to the source. But as a rule they should only use such direct quotes very sparingly – perhaps just once in the whole literature review.

Use of academically credible material (*)

Newspaper articles, popular publications or non-specialist websites can be used as sources but a good quality literature review will also make use of more academic sources. For most projects, a good range of books, websites and journal articles should be used, although some projects may require more in-depth research of a smaller number of texts.

If their school has a subscription to an academic database such as JSTOR, I encourage all students to log on, run a search and identify several academic articles which they can use. Students can also use search engines to find free academic articles online. The directory of open access journals (www.doaj.org) is a good place to start.

Once students have found a really good article, they can use it to help find further good material. If they have found a good source, they should run an author search on an academic database or search engine to see if the author has written anything else that is worth reading. They should look for references to further sources in the bibliographies of the articles they read and the further reading pages of books. I explain to students that researching is a form of detective work: it is all about following threads.

Organization of the literature review

Once the student has assembled information from different sources, they should start to fit the jigsaw pieces into a pattern. What are the main themes that they need to cover? I advise students to write a brief plan, with the headings for the different sections, and then start to slot their material in. This will help them identify gaps requiring further research.

As discussed in Chapter 3, the literature review should be a narrative – a story of the key developments in the field they are researching, which tells us about who did what, where, why and when. Organizing the material into chronological order may make sense. Students may well find that they have several overlapping stories to tell.

Keeping sight of the big picture

Often student researchers get lost in the details of the topic they are studying. So I advise them to include a 'big picture' section at the start of their literature review. In a page or so, they should give a broad-brush sketch of the field within which they are researching. Then they can zoom in to look in detail at the key points that are relevant to their research question. Students will usually be in particular need of guidance from their supervisor at this point. Unless they are very well-read indeed, they will not be in a position to provide an overview of a field of research. It will be helpful to them if their supervisor points them to sources which can provide them with a synoptic overview (e.g. the introduction of a compilation of papers), or a good summary on a free online encyclopedia such as the Stanford Encyclopedia of Philosophy (http://plato.stanford.edu/) or the Internet Encyclopedia of Philosophy (www.iep.utm.edu/).

Academic writing style (*)

The title 'review of literature' can mislead students into writing a series of reviews of each of the sources they have looked at. This isn't the most academic style of writing. They should write about their topic, not about their sources. So instead of saying 'The first source I looked at (Smith and Jones, 2006) said that Einstein was influenced by Hume', they should say something like this: 'Hume's influence on Einstein has been noted (Smith and Jones, 2006).'

The style of writing in the literature review should be formal, not casual. It should be objective in tone, not subjective. The student will not be expressing their own opinion too much (apart from when evaluating sources); the place to do that is in the discussion section. It is worth drawing students' attention to the style of writing used in the journal articles. The best literature reviews are those that have a scholarly feel.

Writing which makes sense

Once they have written their first draft, I ask students to have a look at the entire literature review and ask themselves if it makes sense. They should focus on trying to make it *flow*. This means thinking about the links between paragraphs. Would it make more sense if the sections were in a different order? Are there missing sections they need to add to help it make sense? I remind them that good writing makes things as clear and simple as possible for the reader. They may know a lot about their subject, so it may seem clear and obvious to them. But they are writing for people who *don't* know about their subject. They should always keep the reader in mind.

Supervising the writing of the discussion section

The discussion section is – as the name suggests – a discussion. But it is a discussion of a particular sort. It is an argument. One of the virtues of separating the literature review from the discussion section is that it makes very clear to students that we expect them to argue. Less confident students prefer to go on reviewing what other people have said and often don't get around to putting their own point of view until they reach the conclusion, where it emerges hesitantly. I explain to students that the discussion section is the part of the dissertation in which they state what they believe to be the answer to their research question and argue for it.

The model of philosophical discussion that was described in Chapter 2 can be applied here to provide students with a framework for organizing their writing. A survey of the 'endoxa' – the viewpoints which informed people hold – is a good starting point. Then the student should put their own point of view forward with supporting arguments. They should be encouraged to identify and respond to counter-arguments.

In stronger dissertations, the pattern of argument, counter-argument and response will not simply happen in isolated sections but will be threaded through the whole discussion section. Stronger dissertations usually contain a number of arguments which, taken together, build the case for the main point of view being defended. To assist students in creating this sort of nested argument structure, you may want to ask them to think about the subquestions which they need to answer in order to answer the main research question. The student can then go on to construct argument/counter-argument and response sections for each subquestion.

When developing arguments, students should draw on the material that they have found when doing the research for their literature review.

Good reasoning involves using evidence to provide objective support for the viewpoint being defended. So there should be use of research sources – not, this time, simply in the form of reviewing what people say, but of showing how it provides support for their point of view.

From those capable of climbing to the higher rungs of the ladder of logic (which is by no means all students), you should expect to see identification and response to counter-arguments as part of the discussion. Here, I emphasize that they should be looking for the *strongest* argument against their position. It will not do to knock down a straw man. To build a really robust case, they need to think about the best objections to what they are saying and seek to respond to them.

Planning a discussion

Students find it difficult to get started on their discussion section, since they don't find it easy to construct arguments of their own. Those who lack confidence tend to produce discussion sections that overlap considerably with their literature reviews, offering a few comments on what others have written rather than their own arguments. Others will write in a discursive fashion, talking about the issues in their project and perhaps offering some reasons to support what they are saying, but without developing the central arguments in a sustained way.

To encourage students to develop their own arguments, they need to plan to give their discussion a strong argumentative structure. To help them, I ask them to write a plan in which they consider questions such as:

- What are the main philosophical frameworks which are relevant to your question?
- What is the point of view which you are going to defend in your discussion?
- What philosophical arguments can you give, based on what you have researched, in defence of your point of view?
- Are there subquestions which you need to answer in the process of building up arguments for the main point you are making?
- What are the strongest counter-arguments to your point of view?
- How would you respond to these counter-arguments?

Sometimes, it helps students simply to talk through their ideas – either with their supervisor or with another student. These questions can be used as the basis for an interview, the aim of which is to help the student begin to articulate their ideas and arguments. The interview can then be written up as the basis of a plan for the discussion.

Using frameworks in discussion

In Chapter 2, the suggestion was made that it can be helpful to introduce ethical discussion by means of some initial teaching of key ethical frameworks. The rationale here was that this can assist students in identifying arguments which they come across, and that it can be a useful tool in helping them to organize their own thinking about ethical questions. This teaching technique reflects the plurality of ethical conceptions that exists, and it is consistent with the view that a full-orbed understanding of ethical problems requires an appreciation for the divergent ways of thinking which people bring to such questions.

The idea of using frameworks as an organizing tool is one which can be applied to philosophical problems in other areas as well. With most philosophical questions, there is a range of frameworks which define, in broad outline, the spectrum of opinion within which debate is conducted. These frameworks are the 'isms' of the subject: dualism, materialism, relativism, realism, reductionism, essentialism, and so forth. It can be helpful to introduce students to a number of these frameworks. They can serve as a classificatory tool, which can be applied both when the student is researching and when they are seeking to work out their own ideas.

A reminder about these frameworks can be helpful for students who are struggling to know what to write about in the discussion section of their dissertations. So, for instance, you might suggest to a student who is writing about the ethics of the fur trade that she should research and critically assess arguments drawing on the frameworks of utilitarianism, divine command theory, rights and duties, and virtue ethics.

There is, of course, a danger that using frameworks in this way creates a false impression of simplicity and leads students to miss out on the sophistication of the way a particular philosopher develops their ideas. But that risk can be minimized by ensuring that they are introduced sensibly – with an explanation that they represent a useful starting point, and that students may well decide that the really interesting, worthwhile ideas, do not fit neatly into any of the frameworks.

Using frameworks to organize a discussion

A post-16 student is wondering what to write about for her philosophy project. Her teacher asks her if she has read anything recently. She mentions a book by Jodi Picoult called *My Sister's Keeper*, about a child who was created to be a 'saviour sibling', providing bone marrow for her elder sister, who has leukaemia. They decide this would be a good topic for research. The more the student reads, the more aspects she discovers. She has a discussion with her teacher about how she can organize the threads within the discussion. Her teacher reminds her of the ethics seminar when they looked at four frameworks: consequentialism, rights and duties, divine command theory and virtue ethics. She plans out her discussion with sections corresponding to each of these. In thinking about consequences, she thinks first of all about the consequences for the 'saviour' sibling, as well as for the sister who needs help, and also the parents. She also realizes that there are wider consequences – if one family is allowed to create a designer baby, should others? And on what grounds would it be permissible? When she starts thinking about rights and duties, she realizes that there is a question about the moral status of embryos and about the duties parents have. Do embryos have rights? Do parents have a duty to do all that they can to ensure that their embryos are as healthy as possible? Is it acceptable to create a baby as a means to an end? Her teacher points her to a basic introduction to Kant's moral philosophy, where she learns about the idea that human beings should be treated as ends in themselves, and not as means. But she wonders whether that rule is always followed? Would it, for example, rule out parents deciding to have a second child on the basis that it would be good for their first to have a sibling? And at what stage of development does an embryo acquire the moral status of possessing rights? She finds that when she looks at the perspective of religious believers, many are opposed to the idea of designer babies. There is an argument about 'playing God'. And since the procedure involves the creation by IVF of multiple

⇨

embryos, many religious believers express concern about what will happen to those which are not implanted. Thinking about virtue ethics raises yet more questions. Justice is widely regarded as a cardinal virtue. What is the just thing to do when parents wish to create a saviour sibling by pre-implantation genetic diagnosis? Is it fair to select an embryo on the basis that this embryo will be able to provide bone marrow donations to a sibling? Is it fair to ask a growing child to provide such donations? The use of the ethical frameworks has not made it any easier for the student to decide what the right answer is – but it has helped her to organize her discussion of the issue and given her a sense of the spectrum of ethical opinion.

Balanced discussion

Use of the argument/counter-argument structure should not lead students to assume that they should sit on the fence. Being 'balanced' is sometimes taken to mean giving arguments for and against and refusing to take sides. While this might be appropriate if the evidence really is finely balanced, more often than not, it is a sign that the student is playing safe. I explain to them that they need to stick their neck out and commit themselves to arguing for a particular point of view, while also taking account of the weight of counter-arguments. They will be more likely to learn about the strengths, and weaknesses, of the position they choose to defend if they make a serious attempt at arguing in favour of it. By doing this, they are joining in with the ongoing conversation which we call philosophy.

There is an opposite mistake to be avoided as well, which is to fail to acknowledge that there is something to be learned from those on the opposite side of the debate. I emphasize that students should demonstrate that they have learned something as a result of their study of counter-arguments. Occasionally, a student really does change their mind – and this calls for some serious rewriting. More commonly, though, they begin to feel the force of counter-argument. This can affect them in various ways. It might be that they modify their position, adopting a more qualified stance. Alternatively, they may continue to hold to the same view, but accept that they cannot rely on arguments which they originally thought valid. Change like this is a positive sign: it indicates that the student is really engaged with the project of rational enquiry and is able to learn from counter-argument. It is extremely impressive when you see students who are genuinely moved by the power of philosophical reasoning, particularly if the topic they are writing about is one about which they have strong personal beliefs.

> ### An example project: Could we survive the death of our bodies?
>
> A student (aged 16) is unsure about what question to choose for his philosophy project. In conversation with his teacher, he mentions that he has been thinking about mortality. His teacher suggests he could write his project on the topic. He chooses as his research question: 'Could we survive the death of our bodies?' In his literature review, he examines historical changes in the idea of death, from the spiritual point of view of the ancient world (death as the soul leaving the body) through to a modern definition in terms of cessation of the brain functions that support consciousness. In his discussion section, he maps out arguments for and against survival of bodily death using the frameworks of mind/body dualism and materialism. He argues from a materialist perspective, so his supervisor suggests he carries out an interview with a local clergyman to get a counter-argument.

Topping and tailing

To round off their dissertation, students should write a formal academic conclusion, in which they give a succinct account of what they have argued. The key point here is to tell them that although they may know perfectly well what the main points are, it won't do any harm for the reader to be reminded of them. Helping students become aware of the reader's perspective is a key to helping them develop as writers. It is worth pointing out that the reader may have found the main line of argument hard to follow when first reading it, so a brief summary at the end won't seem repetitive, but will be helpful.

I also ask students to write a short (half page to a page) evaluation of their project. Here, the point is not to write more about the subject matter of their dissertation, but to write about the research process. It is a chance for them to reflect on what they have done well and be honest about weaknesses in their work. I usually suggest, with ever-so-light irony, that given that most philosophical problems have been the topic of debate for several thousand years, it is unlikely that their dissertation will be the last word on the question. So it is worth reflecting on where the gaps in the argument lie. It is impressive when a student has learned enough not simply to be able to put forward a defence of a point of view, but to be able to put their finger on the points where the argument is weakest. This is a sign that they really have climbed the ladder of logic and are beginning to get a sense of what it is really like to do philosophy – to try hard to grapple with some of life's deep, intractable, yet compelling questions and to become aware of the fallibility of our best attempts to provide answers to them.

Finally, I invite students to end with the beginning: to write a brief abstract and an introduction to the dissertation (for pre-16 students, writing shorter dissertations, an abstract can be omitted). Abstract writing is a challenge: can the student capture their entire dissertation in a few hundred words? It is worth taking time to talk to students about what an abstract is. This is a chance to tell them a little about how the academic world works – about the way in which journals work and the importance of using an abstract as a 'trailer' for the project. I also explain to students that they should write their abstract in the present or future tense – not the past tense, which is what they normally do, as they write it last.

While an abstract aims to convey a flavour of the aims, arguments and conclusions of the dissertation, the introduction should focus on the question. It is an opportunity for the student to unpack the question a little: to explore the various philosophical issues that are going to come up in the project. It is also a chance for the student to explain the underpinning motivation for the question – the rationale for asking it. Why is the question a significant one? And why does it matter to them personally? Finally, the introduction should set the scene for the project. In most cases, the philosophical question will emerge out of some events, or developments, within a wider domain. It may be a personal matter, something from the news, or an ongoing controversy (as with many ethical questions and questions about the relationship between science and faith). The introduction is an opportunity for the student to show that they can locate their particular question within a wider domain.

Editing the dissertation

One of the greatest merits of encouraging all students to write a dissertation is that it affords an excellent opportunity to teach them some techniques for improving their writing. It is not simply that they will be writing at greater length. It is that the nature of dissertation writing is such that it calls for a process of drafting and redrafting. This is one of the reasons why it is worth setting a deadline for the first draft of the project well before the final hand-in point. Good writing is a craft and, like any craftwork, the quality of the product depends on how determined the creator has been to go over their work again and again, polishing, smoothing things out, refining and, at times, making drastic cuts.

Good writing is about making the journey smooth for the reader. There should be a clear sense of direction, with signposts throughout (e.g. 'Up until now, I have been reviewing what others have written. Now I will go on to state and defend my own position'). It is worth suggesting that students read their work aloud to see if it makes sense. Are the paragraphs in the right order? Have they included sentences to link one section to the next?

Good writing is also clear writing. I tell students that although philosophy has a reputation for being deep and hard to understand, it is not a virtue if no-one else can make sense of what they have written. The student's dissertation should be comprehensible to a non-specialist. Technicalities should be explained.

I am often asked whether students should write in the first person or the third person. The answer is that it depends which section of the project they are writing. The discussion section is where argument comes. They will be stating their own point of view and saying which arguments they find persuasive. So some use of the first person will be appropriate. The literature review involves reviewing others' work, so will tend to be in the third person ('Smith and Jones reported that . . .'). The introduction will be first personal, as it deals with the reasons for their choice of question, and the conclusion will also be in the first person ('I have argued that . . . Reflecting on the limitations of my argument, I can now see that . . .').

Just keeping going

It is very rare for a student to manage a large-scale dissertation without hitting some problems. One of the major challenges for the supervisor is to help the student keep momentum. As with all aspects of project management, facilitation is the key word. With experience, you will be able to see problems approaching. It may be that the student has started to miss deadlines due to the pressure of other work commitments. Or, perhaps, they are struggling to find suitable source materials, or are finding it hard to make sense of key arguments. Well-timed, supportive intervention can make a huge difference. Project work is a process and one of the main things that students learn is that in any process there are ups and downs. If you are supervising, one of your jobs is to be ready to provide the encouragement and support to get them through the tough patches. Project supervision can be demanding, both in terms of the time it requires and because the supervisor has to think on their feet all the time (no two projects are ever the same!). But when the project comes to completion, it is all the more rewarding to be able to look back and appreciate the valuable lessons about persistence and problem-solving that have been learned on the way.

Reunifying the Curriculum: Encouraging Students to Think Philosophically in All Subject Areas

5

Finding philosophy everywhere

Thus far, we have chiefly been exploring what is involved in teaching and mentoring students philosophically in the context of philosophical discussions and project work. In this chapter, we turn our attention to the wider question of philosophy's relationship to the rest of the curriculum. What can a philosophical approach offer to other subjects?

Most of what students learn in school happens in the context of a curriculum which divides knowledge into discrete subjects. Students tend as a result to have a compartmentalized idea of knowledge. They think about science, in science lessons, and history, in history lessons. What they don't do much of, because there isn't an obvious place for it in the curriculum, is to think about the connections between different subject areas. It is here that philosophy has something to offer. Philosophy can help students to step outside of the curriculum boxes and think about fundamental questions – the general questions that underpin learning in particular areas.

Philosophy is a 'sense-making' activity. It works by addressing the confusion which we feel when we start to think about concepts – the elements of thought. It is an activity which can be carried out in connection with concepts used in any subject. You can do philosophy of history, art, design, religion, science, language, and so on. Whenever you ask about the foundational ideas in each of these subjects, and try to make sense of how concepts work in these areas, you are doing philosophy. It is thus a subject that can be applied to any area of learning.

The fact that a philosophical approach can help to unify the curriculum is not coincidental. If we take a look back over the history of different disciplines, we find that many have emerged from philosophical reflection. Astronomy, cosmology, biology, chemistry, psychology, economics, sociology, linguistics, politics and logic: these all have their roots in philosophical reflection. By drawing attention to the underlying unity at the level of the foundations of knowledge in different disciplines, we both deepen and integrate the educational experience.

We will see that philosophical issues can be located even within subjects that seem, on the face of it, to have nothing to do with philosophy. Admittedly, there may not be a great deal of time for Socratic dialogue in any given subject – but then, it doesn't take long for a gadfly to sting a horse.

The big questions

To appreciate how philosophy can be applied to more or less any subject on the curriculum, we need to think a little more about the nature of philosophy itself. It is the subject in which we consider the 'big questions'. Philosophy concerns itself with the most general questions of all: questions about fundamental ideas, such as those of space, time, cause and effect, reality, knowledge, truth, beauty, goodness, identity, meaning, justice, the mind and the self.

Philosophy exists because when we turn our attention towards these ideas, we realize that we do not understand them well. Consider the idea of space. If asked, we would probably say that we know something about the space around us. We know our way around the area in which we live. Most of us also have some broader geographical knowledge. We know roughly where our home town stands in relationship to the country of which it is a part, and where that country is in relation to the rest of the world. An astronomer could tell us a great deal about the location of the world, relative to the planets and stars which comprise our galaxy. A cosmologist could inform us about the position and motion of our galaxy in relation to the rest of the material universe. It would seem, then, that a great deal is known about space.

But suppose now that we were to ask these questions: What is space? Is it a thing, or is it an absence of things? Would space still be there if all the things in space – moons, planets, stars and galaxies – were to disappear? Is space infinite in extension? Are regions of space infinitely divisible? It is not at all easy to answer these questions. We take ourselves to know a great deal about space – but when we turn our attention to space itself, we find that we don't really understand it at all. We may have answered many questions about space – but we still don't have an answer to the big question of what space really is. Despite our growth in knowledge, we lack understanding.

If a concept like space is baffling, a concept like time is even more baffling still. Saint Augustine drew attention to the philosophically perplexing nature of time when he wrote:

> What, then, is time? I know well enough what it is, provided that nobody asks me; but if I am asked what it is and try to explain, I am baffled. (Augustine, 1961, p. 264)

Time is a familiar enough part of daily life. We talk and think about it without noticing how utterly baffling it is. We say things such as 'Hasn't time flown?' or 'Christmas will soon be upon us' without pausing to consider what they might mean. When we do ask ourselves questions like this, we immediately realize that something which we accepted as a familiar part of life – something which we thought we knew – is in fact completely mysterious. Does time itself move? If it flows, how quickly does it flow? Are future events already real? Are past events still real? Or is only the present real? The difficulty of knowing what to say in response to such questions makes us realize that we don't really know what time is at all.

Many people would rather not trouble themselves too much about problems like this, preferring instead just to get on with their everyday lives. But if there is a Socratic gadfly around, we might find that we are stung into thinking seriously about them. The puzzlement we feel when confronted with the fact that we simply don't understand concepts we use everyday can become the starting point for philosophical enquiry.

Exploring meaning

Socrates – the gadfly – gained his reputation because of his irritating habit of questioning people to show them that they did not understand things as well as they thought they did. Socrates liked to draw attention to the fact that his contemporaries, who were keen to propound theories about justice, truth, and the like, could rapidly be reduced to baffled silence when asked to give a clear account of what they meant by such terms. Professor Myles Burnyeat describes the Socratic method in this way:

> You start with a familiar and important concept – it's always a concept that is important in our lives – and you get people to realise that there are problems in that concept. They try to think about it; they produce an answer. Socrates shows the inadequacy of the answer. You end up not with a firm answer, but with a much better grasp of the problem than you had before. Whether you are a twentieth-century reader or an ancient reader, you have been drawn into the problem; you are left still wanting to get the answer, and feeling that perhaps you can contribute. (Burnyeat in Magee, 1987, p. 16)

Philosophy, understood in this way, is a method: a means of enquiry, not a body of doctrines. It is the quest to try to make sense of fundamental ideas. These ideas are extremely hard to pin down and are a source of confusion for students – and not just students! Ask anyone to name some things they know to be true and they will be able to oblige. But if you were to ask what is *meant* by 'knowledge' and 'truth', then you would be more than likely to receive a bewildered stare. How, then, can we go about tackling the intriguing but troubling questions of philosophy?

Philosophers go about addressing these problems using a technique known as 'conceptual analysis'. This may sound daunting, but in essence the idea is a simple one. To analyse a concept is to explore and attempt to clarify its meaning.

The point here is sometimes misunderstood. Some people think that what philosophers want is a 'definition'. On this view, philosophy is little more than the activity of scribbling 'Define your terms!' in the margin of a student's essay. Definitions, if they can be given, may be a help-ful way of explaining the meaning of a term. But one of the lessons of philosophy is that concepts are not easily pinned down. Many terms do not have single definitions, and even when we have separated out the different senses of a word, we may not have very clear definitions for each of them. What is needed is not so much a formal definition as an *explanation of meaning*. There are various ways in which this can be done. Wittgenstein thought that giving some examples was not at all a bad place to start. Comparisons and contrasts can help too. And there is no harm in looking up dictionary definitions, though these should not be assumed to be authoritative. What is important in philosophical discussion is that the *conceptual* nature of the problems being discussed is properly appreciated, and that students are given some guidance as to how they can go about explaining their ideas more clearly.

Clarifying ideas

The following questions can be asked in order to try to under-stand a philosophical idea which comes up during the course of a discussion:

- Could you just explain what you mean by . . .?
- What do you think are the implications of that idea?
- Would it be fair to express what you are saying in this way . . .?
- Could you give me an example to illustrate what you were saying about . . .?

The importance of semantics

We have an unfortunate habit of treating questions about meaning – semantic questions – as though they were not that important. People talk about a point being 'merely semantic', or say things like, 'That's just a matter of definition.' Philosophy, understood as the activity of addressing conceptual confusion, is sometimes derided as being nothing more than a game played with words. But we should not underestimate the importance of semantic issues. They are central to many of the most important questions of all. This can be seen by considering the following story.

> I am sitting talking to a bright student with a strong religious faith.
>
> 'Can God do things?' I ask.
>
> 'Yes' comes the answer.
>
> 'And are actions events?' – 'I think so'.
>
> 'And do events consist in things changing?' 'That would seem right', he replies.
>
> 'If God exists outside time, he cannot change. In which case, he cannot do anything, since an action would be an event, and an event would involve change. Would you agree?'
>
> The student pauses for a while then says, 'I'm going to have to think about this.'

In this exchange, I am not concerned with the question of whether or not there is a God. I am concerned with a *semantic* question. How are we to understand the concept of a being that exists outside time? Is such an idea compatible with other things people often say about God, such as that He acts in particular ways? I am, in Socratic fashion, challenging the student to start to examine his concept of God.

In terms of philosophical method, concerns about meaning are of paramount significance. We err when we try to resolve questions about the truth of philosophical propositions if we have not first sorted out the semantic issues. This is a point often forgotten in the heat of a debate. One person says something and someone else immediately disagrees. But until the proposition under discussion has been clarified, the debate will generate more heat than light. Arguments about the existence of God are a case in point: there is no point getting into a debate about this without first exploring the concept of God. Leaving central concepts unanalysed is a recipe for confusion.

There have been some philosophers who have held that the *only* task of philosophy is the analysis of language, and that it has no business adjudicating on claims about what really exists. We may not want to take that restrictive view, but we would be well advised to ensure that we do take time to clarify the terms which are in use when philosophical discussion is happening.

The cultivation of understanding

The purpose of engaging in a philosophical exploration of the meaning of ideas is to promote understanding. The cultivation of understanding is a primary goal of education and philosophy has a role to play in helping to achieve this goal. At the risk of slight oversimplification, we can criticize modern, assessment-oriented education for focusing on factual learning at the expense of conceptual understanding. The dominance of facts in education is largely a result of the dominance of an assessment instrument – the written examination – which tends to reward factual recall. We spend a long time ensuring our students' heads are filled with facts – the facts they 'need to know' for their various examinations. A consequence of the dominance of factual learning is that we spend less time than we ought to at the all-important task of exploring the conceptual structure of the knowledge students are acquiring. The result is that students may come to learn a lot of information, but not necessarily gain a great deal of understanding. This is not educationally satisfactory. The cultivation of understanding, rather than the rote learning of facts, should be our goal.

Understanding is not something that can be 'delivered' atomistically and, hence, it is not something encouraged by an assessment culture which is based on discrete learning outcomes and modular assessment. It involves not just knowledge of facts, but a synoptic grasp of the relationship between the elements of what has been taught. This takes time to develop and the right sort of setting. We need time to allow students to think about what they are learning as a whole. The name we give to thought which aims to achieve synopticity – to perceive the logical relations between ideas and to reflect on the meaning of the whole – is philosophy.

To reiterate one of the main theses of this book: this is not to say that philosophy needs to be added to an already crowded curriculum – at least, not wholesale and for everyone. It is to say that, within each subject area, the philosophical framework of that discipline should be allowed to come into focus during the course of learning within that field. Students should be given space to reflect, not just on what they are learning, but on how what they are being taught comes to be regarded as knowledge, and how they can utilize knowledge-creating ways of thinking for themselves. They need time as well to think about the meaning and significance of what they are learning and how it relates to what they have been taught in other subjects.

Poetry, physics and philosophy

I am teaching physics to a group of 17-year-old students. They are beginning a unit about the physics of the nucleus. I write three propositions on the board:

'Nuclear decay is a random process'
'Time future contained in time past'
'We are morally responsible for our actions'

Here we have a fact about nuclear physics, an ethical statement and a line from a poem by T. S. Eliot. I ask the class to tell me the idea which links these three – and I sit back as a barrage of questions and ideas begins to fly. I allow 15 minutes of increasingly frustrated discussion, during which a fair amount of scepticism about the point of the exercise is expressed ('Why are we doing this?', 'Do we need to know this for the exam?', 'Is this on the syllabus?' . . .). But I want them to think. I want them to learn that classical physics is governed by the notion of determinism, according to which there is a sufficient cause (in time past) for every future event – but I want them to *understand* this piece of knowledge in a wider, philosophical and poetic context. I want them to begin to appreciate that scientific determinism has led many people to question whether we are morally responsible for our actions, since if determinism is true, we lack the freedom to do other than we actually do. I want them to understand how significant it is that quantum physics seems to have furnished a counter-example to determinism, in that two nuclear particles, in all other respects identical, can differ just in that one of them decays during a given time interval, and the other does not. I want them to see that physics is not simply a story about matter in motion: it is the story of the universe, and we are included in this universe, so that physics is telling us things about ourselves, if we understand it properly. I want them to realize that the ideas physicists talk about have to be understood within a philosophical context, and, when seen in this light, we can move seamlessly between the world of the physicist and the world of the poet. How else can we properly understand the romantic poets, if not by appreciating their work as a reaction to the enormous power of the deterministic, mechanistic world-picture which the triumph of Newtonian physics seemed to force upon us? And what could the poets of today make of the quantum mechanical world-picture? I want my students to know that nuclear decay is not a deterministic process but most of all, I want them to begin to see how much is contained within a statement of this fact. I want them to begin to understand.

Reuniting the two cultures

Understood as a method of enquiry, philosophy is a subject which can be linked to any other. It thus has a role to play in helping to establish, or re-establish, connections between different subject areas. 'Cross-curricular study' is an ideal which is often acknowledged but which proves difficult to achieve. Philosophy has a valuable contribution to make here. One of the divides which can be bridged by a philosophical approach is that described by C. P. Snow, in his famous lecture on 'The two cultures': The division between the arts and the sciences.

Despite attempts to encourage a more holistic approach, it remains the case, in the United Kingdom at least, that many students after the age of 16 still go down 'science' or 'humanities' routes. Even when their options do involve both, there is little opportunity for exploring questions in an integrated, genuinely cross-curricular fashion.

Science students tend not to be strong in areas that humanities students specialize in. They lack skills in critical reading of sources and in constructing arguments of a philosophical nature. They may also lack confidence to take part in discussion and debate, or present their ideas. Conversely, humanities students may be strong in the area of critical reading, discussion and debate, but lack a confident awareness of science, and feel unsure how to go about engaging in the important discussions going on in the public domain about science's ethical impact. They are drawn to these questions, but need support in order to be able to access the relevant scientific knowledge.

A programme in which science is studied philosophically has a significant role to play in breaking down the divide which C. P. Snow identified. It helps science students to appreciate that there is a 'human face to science', and that their understanding of science can be deepened by studying it from historical and philosophical standpoints. Conversely, it provides a means of helping humanities students to develop their 'scientific literacy': of enabling them to continue to think about and engage with science. We have here an example of how the synoptic power of philosophy can help to break down some of the walls which artificially divide the world of learning.

A philosophical approach to cross-curricular study

As an example of the importance of fostering cross-curricular thought along philosophical lines, consider the issue of animal testing. This might come up as a discussion topic in a biology lesson. The issue, though, can only really begin to be understood with the combined resources of science, history and philosophy. It needs to be examined from the standpoint of science, since we need to know about the nature of the tests and their potential utility. The ethical assumptions which underpin arguments on either side of the debate will need philosophical examination. Other branches of philosophy are relevant as well. It is necessary to think about the nature of animal minds. Do animals suffer? Most of us would not doubt that they do, though some influential philosophers, most notably Descartes, thought of animals as 'mere automata'. But there remains a question about the nature of animal suffering. If animals lack the conceptual resources to think about their experiences – again, an assumption about which science and philosophy will have something to say – then there will be a clear, and ethically relevant, difference between the nature of animal pain and pain as it occurs in most humans – where, for instance, there is a capacity to remember, as well as to anticipate distressing episodes.

Science, ethics and the philosophy of mind, then, will all be relevant. History is relevant as well. One feature of the argument about animal testing is that the division between proponents and opponents is deep-seated. Properly to understand a dispute such as this, students need to understand why people adopt different, and sometimes radically opposed, ethical standpoints. For that, a study of the history of ideas is necessary. The impact of Christian theology on ethical thought will need to be explored, as well as the rise, in recent times, of the animal rights movement. Those who think that the interests of animals should be given the same regard as the interests of humans accuse their opponents of an ethical failing called 'speciesism', a term which has been deliberately chosen to call to mind the ethical failings of sexism and racism. Understanding such a line of thought calls, then, for a study of the currents in ethical and political thinking that underpin this sensitivity about unjustified discrimination against those who differ from oneself – either by race, gender or species. A question such as 'Should we test cosmetics on animals?' might well start out being explored in a classroom discussion in a biology lesson, but the depth and complexity of the issue means that, for it to be properly understood, a cross-curricular approach involving history, ethics, philosophy and politics (and perhaps other subjects as well) is necessary.

Exploring the philosophical dimension of different subjects

Curriculum time is precious, but it is worth spending some time within each subject exploring its philosophical dimension, even if the main aim of the teacher is not to go very far down the philosophical road. In such settings, a little philosophy can act as a stimulant to thought. It catalyses the reaction which goes on inside the mind of students when they begin to sense that something strange and interesting is going on, something which is worth thinking about some more.

The exploration of philosophy within the context of different disciplines does not call for an elaborate philosophical scheme of work to be developed by each teacher. It is a matter of using the occasional lesson, or even just part of a lesson, to make a foray into the world of philosophy. These philosophical interludes may consist of no more than asking stimulating questions, or holding brief discussions, but they have the potential to spark curiosity and suggest avenues for further enquiry.

It may be helpful for a teacher with specialist knowledge of philosophy to assist here, either by advising on the planning of a lesson with a philosophical theme, or by team-teaching or a lesson-swap arrangement. But with a few pointers towards the right sort of starting point, and some suggested activities, all staff can facilitate such sessions.

Opportunities for philosophy across the curriculum

Philosophy can be threaded into the curriculum at many points. Here are some possibilities:

- Individual teachers can include philosophical discussions in their lessons.
- A programme can be organized in which a philosophical theme is explored within different subjects across the course of a term. There are general concepts such as 'truth', 'belief', 'fact', 'opinion', 'creation', 'discovery' about which many subjects have something to say. Asking students to think about how the same idea appears within different subjects is a way of starting to break down the divides between disciplines.
- To allow for more in-depth exploration, a collapsed timetable day can be given over to philosophical enquiry. A topic such as 'What is the mind?' can be explored through a programme of short talks in which teachers of different subjects explain the topic from their point of view, with group discussion seminars in-between. One good activity to include in such a day is the 'opinion spectrum', in which a number of different philosophical perspectives are described, then students are invited to identify where they stand on the spectrum, and then discuss the reasons they would give for their opinion. Alternatively, students can be given the chance to respond creatively, with mind-maps, posters or short devised pieces of performance work, exploring some of the ideas raised during the day.

Entry points to the world of philosophy

A good way in which to draw students' attention to philosophical issues is to take a concept that is used all the time when teaching a particular subject, and devote some time during a lesson to exploring its meaning. For example, questions such as 'What is beauty?', 'What is meaning?' or 'What is truth?' could be explored within the context of an art, language or science lesson.

A discussion of questions such as these is a good 'entry point' to the world of philosophical enquiry. The aim of the discussion need not be to establish a fixed definition of these terms, but rather to explore their meaning; to think about examples of how they are used, to contrast different usages and to highlight interesting ambiguities and problems within the concepts. In order to help a class engage with these abstract ideas, it is best to use some subject-specific stimulus material to get the discussion going (see Table 5.1 for some suggestions). There is potential for cross-curricular links to be made here too, by comparing and contrasting the use of these concepts in different subjects.

Table 5.1 Philosophical problems and subjects where they can be explored

Philosophical Problem	Subject Areas	Possible Stimulus Material
What is space?	Geography, Physics Art	Maps created using different projections Photographs of an empty beach and the same beach full of sunbathers. A picture of the medieval universe withthe earth at the centre and the heavens above. The COBE microwave map of the entire universe A picture of an empty room in the Tate Modern
What is time?	History, Physics	Philosophical paradoxes about time (Zeno's paradoxes, McTaggart's paradox, the twin's paradox) HG Wells *The Time Machine*
What is the self?	English, History, Psychology	*Hamlet* Case studies of multiple personality disorder and other cases of abnormal psychology The bundle theory of the self

(Cont'd)

Table 5.1 Continued

Philosophical Problem	Subject Areas	Possible Stimulus Material
What is the mind?	Psychology	The story of Phineas Gage Newspaper reports of neuroscientific discoveries
What is free will?	Religious Studies, Psychology	A report of the work of Benjamin Libet A clip from the film *Minority Report* The debate between libertarianism and compatibilism
What is logic?	Science, Mathematics, Computing	Elements of propositional logic Common fallacies The problem of induction
What is knowledge?	All	Clips from *The Matrix* Descartes' *Meditations*, chapter one
What is truth?	All	The game 'Eleusis' A class debate: Is truth created or discovered?
What is beauty?	Art and Design, Media Studies, History	A comparison of Rubens portraits of women and contemporary supermodels A class debate about whether beauty is more than 'skin-deep'
What is meaning?	Languages, Psychology	The question: Is your idea of 'blue' the same as mine? Wittgenstein's 'Beetle in the box' thought experiment
What is the difference between right and wrong?	All	Brainstorm to generate a list of ethical dilemmas Introduce common ethical frameworks Apply these in discussing dilemmas
What is happiness?	Psychology, Religious Studies	Brainstorming the ingredients of happiness Research into the findings of studies of happiness Compare and contrast: happiness, well-being and pleasure

An electronic version of this table, complete with hyperlinks to possible stimulus material, is available on the companion website.

Foundational questions

Thinking philosophically means asking questions about the foundations of a subject (see Chapter 3, 'Thinking more deeply'). We are going

to explore a number of questions that arise in connection with the foundations of specific subjects on the curriculum. These questions can be used in a number of different ways:

- You might use them to start a class debate.
- They could form part of a mock interview for a student preparing for university entrance.
- You might ask students to write a structured essay, in which they explore the meaning of one of these questions, state a point of view, give arguments, then consider and respond to counter-arguments. (An exercise like this forms part of some thinking skills aptitude tests.)
- If students find a particular question very stimulating, you could suggest they use it as the basis for a philosophical project.
- But you might not want to do much more than raise the question and let it hang in the air.

History

The concepts used in history are a rich source of philosophical puzzles. Questions which can be explored include the following:

Is the past real? According to a view called presentism, only the present moment exists. Nothing of the past exists, apart from traces in the present (our memories and records of past events). If these traces were to be destroyed, there would be absolutely nothing of the past left. Suppose that there are no historical records which will tell us whether Caesar crossed the Rubicon. Then the sentence 'Caesar crossed the Rubicon' is empty – it is neither true nor false. Alternatively, some hold that the past is real: that sentences such as this one about Caesar are now true or false in virtue of what happened, regardless of whether we will ever be able to determine their truth or falsity. What, then, should we say about the reality of the past? Is it only real insofar as it leaves detectable traces in the present?

What is an historical fact? The debate about whether the past is real leads into a further question about facts. According to some philosophers, facts are solid, concrete elements of reality. They are what make true sentences true. The facts are out there. They really exist. But according to others, there are no objective facts. 'Facts' are what we relate when we tell stories. A fact is part of a narrative. They do not exist objectively. We make the world through our language.

How we think about facts will make a significant difference to the way we understand what historians do. If facts are objective elements of reality, then history becomes a process of enquiry. Like science, history involves searching for a theory which makes best sense of the facts. But if there are no objective historical facts, history becomes a matter of subjective personal interpretation. We each create our own story about the past, and there is no objective criterion for deciding which of these stories is true. Should we then give up the idea of history as a form of enquiry which aims to find the truth about the past? Are there alternatives to the objectivist and subjectivist positions?

Can history uncover causes? We are fascinated by the question of what makes things happen. What makes us tick? And what forces are at work to shape the flow of the events of history? In Chapter 3, we saw how a question about the causes of the First World War could lead naturally into a philosophical question about the possibility of knowledge of historical causes. When we begin to think about this, we quickly see that the idea of causation is a problematic one. We are naturally inclined to think that events have causes, but should we? Do events in history unfold in a deterministic way? Or could events happen even though there was nothing preceding them which made them happen? Is history made up of deterministic processes or is it a realm of contingency and happenstance?

Languages

Language and the way in which it is used is a central element within philosophy, and language lessons – whether English or a modern foreign language – provide a good starting point from which to enter philosophical territory. The following are topics which can be explored here:

How do words get their meaning? How do words and the world relate? How do words get their meaning? Is the meaning of a word an object which it stands for? If every phone box in the world were to vanish tomorrow, would 'phone box' still mean something? If so, what would it mean? And what about words which don't stand for particular items? Do words like 'love' also get their meaning by standing for things? And what about those uses of language which aren't descriptive? How do orders, promises or requests get their meaning?

Is reality something we make through our language? Linked to these questions is a question about the priority of language and reality. Which comes first? Is it right to think that there is a world out there, which exists regardless of how we speak or think about it? Or is the world shaped by our language? Or could both be true? Could there be 'socially constructed' realities, as well as objective realities which don't depend on us in any way?

Is meaning an idea in your mind? John Locke proposed a theory of meaning in which the meaning of a word was an idea in the mind of the speaker. This seems initially sensible. We talk about 'sharing ideas' with other people. Many students find the suggestion that the meaning of a word like 'blue' is an idea within the mind is a plausible one. But given that we cannot see inside someone else's mind, does this mean that we can never grasp someone else's meaning? How can we be sure that the idea that we associate with a word is the same as the idea that someone else associates with it?

What is femininity?

In an English class, the question of female identity is discussed. A post-16 student decides she would like to research it further. She chooses 'Is there an essence to femininity?' as her research question. She explores the history of attitudes towards femininity and key events in the rise of feminism in her literature review. For the discussion, her teacher suggests that she makes use of the distinction between essentialist and constructionist frameworks. Essentialists hold that there are characteristics that all women have, which define their femininity. Constructionists argue that female identity is a matter of a socially determined role. She uses these two frameworks in her discussion. After further reading and discussion with her teacher, she begins to wonder whether the truth is best understood as lying neither with constructionism nor with essentialism. This proves to be a fruitful question to ask. It leads her to think about how language works and whether there might be an alternative to the dichotomy between 'fixed essences' and 'socially constructed roles'.

Science

There is a close connection between science and philosophy. Both are subjects in which we enquire into how the world really is. We can move from science into philosophy by looking at some of the following fundamental questions raised by science:

What is scientific knowledge? We place a great deal of confidence in science. But science seems to make universal claims based on particular observations. Isn't that a little risky? How can we be sure that general conclusions based on a finite set of observations are correct? The history of science shows that apparently secure theories have often turned out to be mistaken. Should we be more cautious in what we claim to know?

How is a scientific way of understanding the world related to non-scientific perspectives? For some people, the ultimate explanation for events is not scientific but religious. Yet for many scientists and philosophers, the progress which science has made vindicates the claim that the scientific world-view provides the best way to understand reality. Who is right? Given the success of science in finding explanations, should we conclude that, eventually, it will explain everything? Or are there events which cannot be explained scientifically? If there are, could they be explained in a non-scientific way?

How do science and ethics link? It has been traditional to distinguish between statements of fact and statements of value. But recently, philosophers have called the 'fact-value' distinction into question. There are, it is claimed, facts about how we ought to live. Some would claim that ethics can be studied scientifically – that science could tell us answers to the question 'How should we live?' Is that correct? Should ethics be based on science? If not, what should it be based on?

Psychology

There are many links between philosophy and psychology. Here are a few:

What is the relationship between the mind and the body? Is the mind the same as the brain? Or is it a separate entity which could survive the destruction of the body? Or is it more like a product of the brain? Is it a mistake to think of the mind as a 'thing' at all? Is having a mind better thought of as a capacity for certain sorts of action? If so, which? The way in which these questions are answered will affect the way we think about topics such as mental illness. Should we see mental illness as essentially a matter of malfunctioning brain processes? Or should it be seen as a spiritual problem, as it has been historically, and still is, in some cultures? Or is it best thought of as a phenomenon which has to be understood at many different levels?

What is consciousness? A central aspect of the mind–body problem is the problem of consciousness. To be conscious is to be aware, and, for adult humans, at least when they are wide awake, there is a capacity for self-consciousness; a capacity for being aware that we are aware. We can, introspectively, consider what it is like to have experiences of the world. We can give attention to the blue of the sky, to the pressure of the seat beneath us, to the sound of the breeze outside, and the like. How are we to understand these conscious experiences? Are they only known 'from the inside', as it were? Does it make sense to describe these rich, subjective experiences of the world as simply the firing of neurons inside our brains? How widespread is consciousness? Do animals have it? What about newborn infants or embryos inside the womb? Could consciousness be created in a machine? Is it something that can exist in different degrees? Are there things going on inside our minds of which we cannot be conscious? If there is an unconscious domain to the mind, how important is it? Is it the true seat of our emotions and desires?

Why do we do the things we do? The explanation of action is a deeply perplexing area. When asked to explain our actions, we usually give reasons. But are these reasons best understood as the things which made us act? Are reasons causes? Or is it the case that something else made us act, and the reason is the way in which we help to make sense of what it is that we have done? But if reasons are not the causes of our actions, what are? Presumably the causes of actions are events which occur within our bodies – inside our brains, perhaps. Does this mean that the proper answer to the question, 'What made you do that?' is: 'I don't know?' Does it mean that a scientist is better placed to explain why we do the things we do than we are?

Is there such a thing as a free action? We also like to think that we do some things freely: although we choose to act in one way, it is nevertheless true to say that we might have acted differently. I may have chosen to drink a cappuccino, but I could have ordered an expresso. But is this really true? Are the choices we make free in a significant sense? If the choice we made involved a process going on in our brain, can we really be said to be in control of it? What makes us confident that we could have acted differently? What about cases of people whose behaviour is affected by addictive cravings – are they free? Can we say of them that the things that they choose are what they want? Could it be that they have desires, but that they don't want to have those desires? How is our freedom related to our genetic make-up? Are there behavioural traits which have a genetic cause? If there are, does the causation operate in a way which removes freedom?

Economics and business studies

There are questions here which arise from the nature of economics and also from the ways in which economic knowledge is used.

What is economics? Is economics best understood as a scientific discipline? If it is, does this mean that economic theories are tested in the way theories of physics are tested? How significant is the fact that among the objects of economic study are people who are themselves influenced by economic ideas? Does this feedback loop create a problem for the idea that objective knowledge is possible here? Can economic theories such as game theory explain real world events?

Are the things economics talks about real? The world of economics is full of things which don't seem to exist in the same way that physical objects do: things like exchange rates, balance of payments, gross national product, interest rates and stock market trends. Yet these things seem to affect our lives profoundly. Are they real or not? Do they only exist because we think that they exist? What is money? It isn't just pieces of paper or pieces of gold – it can exist in many forms. But what is it that all these forms share? How valuable is money? What gives it the value that it has?

How is economics related to ethics? How should we distribute the goods which result from economic productivity? If £1 can make a vastly greater difference to the happiness of a person in a less economically developed country than it could to someone in our own, is there an ethical argument for redistributing wealth to poorer countries? Ethics deals with ideas such as welfare: can these be measured using economic indicators? If so, is economics directly relevant to ethics? How should we address dilemmas in which economic values are weighed against ethical values? Is it better for a company to sacrifice profitability for the sake of producing less environmentally damaging products? Is the primary duty of a company to make a profit for its shareholders or to act in an ethical manner? Can a company compete if it prioritizes ethical actions?

Religious studies

Religious studies is a field rich with philosophical questions.

What do people mean when they use the word 'God'? The concept of God is central to the great monotheistic religions, which are followed by the majority of the world's believers. Yet, as some of those believers themselves would accept, it is a concept shrouded in mystery. God is said to be a personal being, yet lacks the attributes of embodiment. His knowledge is said to be unlimited, as is his power and goodness. Each of these ideas generates an entire series of philosophical questions. Is it possible for a person to exist without a body? Does it make sense to speak about a person who is 'present everywhere'? If God has no physical characteristics, how is he able to interact with the physical universe? If he is beyond time and change, how can he do the deeds which are ascribed to him in the scriptures? And, of course, there is the problem of how his perfection is to be reconciled with the imperfection of the world which is termed his creation.

How does religious language work? Theologians who have addressed the problem of making sense of language that is intended to refer to a transcendent realm have offered various models of how it works. Straightforward literalism is obviously problematic. Such a view may once have been believed and it does at least have the merit of making intelligible sense of some of what is said about the divine being. But it does so at the cost of rendering these propositions false. God does not literally speak, having no mouth; he does not literally hear, having no ears and he does not literally have a strong arm which he occasionally stretches out to rescue his people. How, then, are we to understand these statements about God? At this point, one model is that of metaphor, or analogy. Religious language may be a way of gesturing towards what God is: a way of saying what he is like, without ever pinning down his essential being. Alternatively, some radical theologians have suggested that we should not see religious language as descriptive at all; it is 'expressive'. To say that God is love is not to ascribe a property to a mysterious being. It is to express something about the ultimate value of love. It is like saying, 'Love is divine'. But this suggests that much of what the religious believer is saying could, once understood, be agreed with by the non-believer. Is that the right conclusion to draw?

What is the relationship between faith and reason? Can we reason about mysteries such as the nature of the divine being? Philosophy involves the application of critical reason to questions of a fundamental nature. But there are theologians who wish to put reason back in its box. Here, the questions are questions of faith. The fact that we cannot give a rational foundation for the assertions of religion tells us something about ourselves: that our 'reason' is a weak, fallible thing, incapable of probing into questions about the ultimate nature of things. We are in the position of children, who have to take things on trust, and whose insistent 'Why?' questions must often remain unanswered. But where does this leave the project of trying to make sense of the world? If the 'faith card' can be played in a way which immunizes religious doctrines from rational criticism, what is to stop anyone making the same move, in the ethical or political arena, so as to silence unwelcome questioning?

Art and design

In the assessment world, it is sometimes stated that art and design are different. That may be so, but once we dig beneath the surface, we find once again that creative arts also build on philosophical foundations:

What is art? The roots of art lie in the human condition: from the time of the cave painters onwards, we have felt the urge to express ourselves creatively. Is there a single idea which unifies these creative activities? Is there something which all forms of art share? Does art have an essence? Or is it better thought of as a range of different but overlapping activities? If we don't think that there is an essence to art, does this mean that 'anything goes'? Is the concept sufficiently flexible for us to define art as 'anything that anyone has ever considered a work of art (Carey, 2005, p. 29)? Is it part of the task of art to challenge its own definition and to reinvent itself? Is something turned into a work of art by being looked at in a particular way, or by being placed in a particular setting (e.g. a gallery)? These are excellent philosophical questions to ask, and they have a direct bearing on the activities of artists and designers, inviting them to think about whether what they are doing *counts* as art – and if so, why.

Is there such a thing as artistic value? When paintings change hands for millions of dollars, what is it that is being valued so highly? Is there such a thing as the value of an artwork? By what criteria do we distinguish between better and worse works of art? Are these criteria objective? Could someone mistakenly judge a great piece of art to be worthless, or a worthless piece to be great? Do the standards of greatness change over time? Does it make sense to look for something within a picture – proportion, beauty or the quality of the workmanship – to find clues as to the quality of the art? Or is it simply a matter of its effect on viewers? Are some people better equipped than others to judge the value of a work of art?

How are art and design linked to ethics? Are there ethical boundaries which artists and designers should respect? How are they to be drawn? Does art have a special role in challenging the norms of a society? Is it bound always to be ethically controversial? Is an artwork ethically good or bad in itself, or is it a matter of how it is used? Is there a two-way relationship here? Does artistic creation provide a helpful metaphor for ethics? Are ethical values things which we create? Should we, following Nietzsche, see the process of living as being like creating a work of art? Is artistic creativity one of the most fundamental of all human characteristics?

Philosophy and vocational education

In emphasizing the breadth of the conception of philosophically enriched education that I am advocating, it is worth exploring the applicability of this method to vocational education. There have been efforts in recent years to elide the distinction between academic and vocational learning, and to promote 'parity of esteem'. Why shouldn't a qualification in hairdressing be treated as of equal value to one in history? Aren't those who reject parity of esteem just reflecting a deep-seated intellectualist prejudice in our national psyche?

As a philosopher, I am on the side of intellectual enquiry. But I also think that things would be better if we didn't feel the need to pick sides. My own approach has been to explore how a capacity for reflective, philosophical thought can be developed and drawn out within applied contexts. The grain of sand around which the pearl of philosophical thought forms can come from many places.

I had a conversation about this with a colleague in the careers department of the school where I teach. I was musing about the usefulness of philosophical discussion as an element in the education of all young people. 'There is the argument about thinking skills', I said, 'but really, how helpful will all these philosophical discussions be to a young person who is going to become a hairdresser?' 'But remember that hairdressers don't just cut hair', my colleague replied. 'They talk all day to their clients. If a hairdresser has learned at school to be interested in ideas and enjoys discussing them – well, you are going to enjoy talking to them, and that means you will probably go back to them next time you want your hair cut.'

So there you have it: philosophy really does have something for everyone. For hairdressers and historians alike, as a preparation for life, there could not be anything more worthwhile than cultivating among young

Figure 5.1 A philosophical haircut

people the dispositions of curiosity, critical thinking and enjoyment of the discussion of what life is all about (see Figure 5.1).

Philosophy for plumbers

Not all will be philosophers. That is true, but it remains the case that it is the capacity for critical, reflective, evaluative, sense-making thought that is of central importance. And this is just as much the case in good art or design, music-making, or performance work. We want to encourage work in which there is evidence of thought; of consideration, of reflection on influences and the significance of the subjective aspect that the creator brings to the work. Aristotle was not wide of the mark when he noted that rational thought is the human differentia. It is this element that should underpin and direct the successful application of technical skill. To the extent, then, that the factor that underpins and unifies all education is rational thought, all students may not be philosophers, but they can all profit from doing a little philosophy.

That may sound too high-minded. What use is a philosophical approach to students busily working towards a vocational qualification in, say, plumbing? But two points can be made here: first, there is a type of practical autonomy which is possessed by the technician who not only can use techniques he has been taught, but also can adapt, innovate, improvise on, extend and improve those techniques – and that takes the faculties of critical thought, as well as the capacity for reflective evaluation. Secondly, consider that in a fast-changing world, we educators cannot afford to think of ourselves as preparing our charges for one particular vocational way of life. They will be expected to learn again, during the course of their working life, and those best equipped to flourish will be the ones with the facility and confidence to re-engage with learning, as well as with the reflective awareness of the changes in their working environment that presage the need to move in a new direction. In short, no-one can be regarded as well educated who has not been given some help in how to locate working life within life's wider projects.

6

Assessment Reassessed: An Education-Driven Assessment Model

'Existence is not an examination'

I saw this slogan daubed on a wall behind a college in Oxford during my student days. I absolutely agree with the sentiment, but, alas, the reality for so many of our students is very different. Assessment by means of written examination plays a larger role in the lives of young people than it has ever done. The weight of the assessment burden has unbalanced the educational system.

In this chapter, we will see what can be done to redress the balance. I will be arguing in favour of continuous assessment by means of project work. Project work is of considerable educational value, and this value is enhanced if we recognize good quality work by well-constructed, rigorous assessment criteria and thereby encourage students to take this work seriously. I will not be addressing the details of how to assess – this is well covered in guidance from the awarding bodies about project qualifications. But I will explore some of the principles of continuous assessment of projects, and show how a well-thought-out assessment model can help to enhance the learning process. I will also address some of the common criticisms of continuous assessment.

This much can be done within the educational system as it now exists to counter the trend towards teaching-to-the-test and rote-learning for exams. But the implications of the philosophical approach to the curriculum that I have been arguing for go wider. The key concept of 'understanding', and the fact that it has a holistic character, has evident implications for an assessment system in which examinations are largely modularized. We will see that there are good philosophical and pedagogical reasons for moving towards a system in which assessments are less modular in scope, and in which synoptic examination plays a greater part.

These two themes – the value of continuous assessment and the value of general education – jointly support the argument I have been making in this book that a programme of cross-curricular, philosophically based study followed by project work should be something which all students experience at some stage in their journey through secondary education. The case for a philosophical curriculum has been made in detail in recent years (see the papers in Hand and Winstanley, 2009). I am inclined to agree with the view that it should be a compulsory part of the pre-16 curriculum, as it addresses the need to equip students to think and research for themselves, and provides a context within which they can begin to think outside of the curriculum boxes. A similar programme should be available to all students at post-16 stage, and they should be given every encouragement to take it – though in keeping with the structure of provision of post-16 education in the United Kingdom at least, we may not want to make it compulsory.

We also have to address the issues arising from the fact that in contemporary education, assessment feeds into accountability measures. My principal aim in this book is to show how richer, liberal, philosophically enlightened education can happen despite the presence of the bureaucratic apparatus of accountability. But if, as I do, you feel that the most important educational challenge is to get students to think again, you will probably also feel that, to put it mildly, our educational system could do more to encourage this sort of thing. So we will spend some time examining the philosophical argument against the assumption that underpins so much of modern educational practice – that it is measurable outcomes that really matter. First, though, we turn to the things that worry people about continuous assessment.

Common concerns about continuous assessment

Concerns about continuous assessment centre on issues of quality control. How confident can we be about work that has been produced over a period of time, outside of the classroom, potentially with help from family or friends – or via an online service which offers, for the right fee, to do the work on the student's behalf? Within the classroom, isn't it possible for a teacher to be overly directive about the assignments, and effectively do the work for the students? Even when the candidate has not been 'assisted' in these ways, given the ease with which information can be found with the aid of a good search engine, the problem of plagiarism looms large.

We can add further concerns about the way in which project work is marked. How can we be sure that different assessors are operating to the same standard? Isn't a system which relies on the judgement of the teacher open to obvious abuse?

These risks exist, but there is a great deal that can be done by way of careful design of the continuous assessment regime, and guidance about how it should be administered, to safeguard against them. We will look at how concerns about quality control and standardization can be met in this way.

Quality control concerns

The first point to note is that one of the problems with conventional 'coursework' is that there is a great risk of collusion or plagiarism if many students write projects on the same topic. This was in fact a problem that emerged with coursework in one particular UK qualification in 2006, which led to the recommendation that coursework should be done under 'controlled conditions'.

Controlled assessment is in many ways the antithesis of work on a personally chosen topic. The constraining effect of the rules for the implementation of these assessment exercises means that, as an assessment instrument, it tends to reproduce some of the same features we have identified as problematic with exams: sterile hoop-jumping and a complete lack of scope for individual, creative exploration. By contrast, with the project approach we have been exploring, the whole point is to encourage students to write on a topic that they have chosen for themselves. They are expected to select and refine their own research question. While this does not of course prevent them accessing inappropriate sources of help, it does cut down the risk of the entire project being taken from someone else.

The risk of plagiarism can also be reduced if there is close, regular monitoring of the process of production of the work. This can be built in by, for example, operating with a system in which the project contains sections, each of which are written and assessed against their own criteria. The assessor can then monitor the production of these sections and review the work at draft stage. This further reduces the risk that the work will be downloaded or simply cut and pasted from websites. It does not take much training to help assessors to spot work which students have not produced themselves, and guidance about this is easily available.

Assessment criteria can be written so as to reward students who conduct the research process well. So, for instance, the criteria for assessing a literature review differentiate between students who have referenced their work appropriately and those who have not, and between those who have based their project on a wide range of sources and those who have relied too heavily on a few. Students can be asked to submit logs written during the research process, and assessors asked to make judgements, supported by evidence, of how well students managed their work throughout the project process – thereby again safeguarding against students who try to subvert the system by handing in a polished piece of someone else's work just before the deadline.

Another example of how quality control checks can be built into a scheme of continuous assessment is by the inclusion of an oral presentation component, with a question and answer session in which the student is expected to take questions from their assessor. This is an excellent way of judging the quality of the student's understanding of the material presented in their written work. It can serve to confirm an assessment decision – or it can raise concerns which lead the assessor to review the authenticity of what has been submitted.

With major projects, the fact that students are being taught about protocols for source citation and referencing becomes an opportunity to teach them about what plagiarism is, and why it is taken so seriously in the academic community. In the United Kingdom, the Joint Council for Qualifications provides detailed advice to teachers about plagiarism (JCQ, 2008). It is a teacher's responsibility to ensure that students receive detailed information about this. The rules which students are expected to follow are backed up by a rigorous procedure of scrutiny by the awarding bodies, and students are warned of sanctions, which can go so far as disqualification.

In cases where the regulations about appropriate use of sources are not followed, the offence is not always an intentional one. Students may not have understood the protocols for appropriate use of other people's work. When it comes to issues of academic malpractice, prevention is better than cure. With clear instructions to students about how they should go about using research sources, and what counts as acceptable assistance, it is possible not just to safeguard the robustness of the assessment regime, but to turn what could be a problem area into a teaching opportunity.

It is this last point which I think most teachers who make use of continuous assessment would echo. We want to use continuous assessment because it is the best way to assess the sort of activities which we know students learn from – project work, extended assignments, and the like: work which allows scope for development over time and which is not constrained by the dictats of a specification. We know that such assessment requires a higher degree of trust in the teacher, who has to act as the assessor, but we hold that this trust is well placed, as we take our professional duties as assessors seriously. Contrary to what some newspaper reports occasionally like to suggest, teachers are not out to subvert the assessment system.

Students need to learn about how to conduct project work properly. If they go on to higher education (HE), they will quickly find out that there are severe penalties for academic offences involving assessed work. Teachers who prepare students for HE need to give them the best training they can for the sorts of assessment they will face there. In this respect, academics commend qualifications such as the Extended Project Qualification as a valuable component in equipping students for the challenge they will face in HE. In 2008, the PoS programme (a history and philosophy taught course which is assessed by means of the Extended Project) was launched at a conference at Rugby School, where I teach, and which was one of more than 30 schools which piloted the course. Professor Niall Ferguson, one of the keynote speakers at the conference, remarked on the way in which the programme could help students:

> Five years of teaching in American universities have con-
> vinced me that English secondary education has two fun-
> damental weaknesses. There is still too much reliance on
> exam-based assessment, which encourages cramming
> and learning by rote. And the A-level system perpetuates
> the fatal 'two cultures' divide between Arts and Sciences.
> That's one reason that even stars from the best British
> schools find the going tough at Harvard. They're not ready
> for continuous assessment. And they're not ready to spend
> the morning on literature and the afternoon on physics.
> The appeal to me of the Extended Project, as exemplified
> by the Perspectives on Science course pioneered at Rugby,
> is that it offers a cure for both these problems.

Of course there are risks associated with this form of assessment. But then, there are risks associated with examined assessment as well. No system is immune from human fallibility. The news each summer brings its share of 'horror stories' of mistakes on exam papers, impossible questions, the ritual concern about grade inflation and, occasionally, malpractice. Moreover, the main argument of this book is that the way in which we assess exerts an inexorable pressure on the way we teach, and in this regard, our current exam-heavy regime needs to be reviewed. If we are serious about encouraging students to develop capacities such as creativity, deeper, more reflective, more analytical thinking and a capacity to gain a synoptic sense of how a domain of learning links to others, we need to make use of ways to assess these capacities. Written examinations, with questions constrained by a specification, a short time period during which responses have to be produced, and, increasingly, a tendency for questions which can be marked in a mechanical fashion against a predetermined mark scheme, simply don't provide the right tool for making judgements about these qualities. We need a system in which both terminal and continuous assessment have their place.

Let me add one further consideration in favour of continuous assessment. This is related to a theme that has emerged at various points in the argument of this book, namely, that education should be a preparation for life. If we think about life once students leave formal education, then it is clear that assessment continues to play a big part. They will have projects to complete as part of working life. There will be interviews. There will be audits, appraisals and inspections with feedback on their performance, or the performance of departments of which they are a part. Occasionally, too, there might be some professional examinations – for chartered accountants, architects, and the like. But if we compare the amount of examined assessment to the amount of continuous assessment, it is clearly the latter that tends to dominate. Most of the assessment which we all face throughout life involves judgements made about the level of skill we have shown, the extent of our project management skills, the quality of our arguments, or the degree of originality and initiative we have shown. They address our competences and our capabilities. So we might well feel that it would be worth exploring how to bring assessment within education more into line with the way that it is done during most of the rest of life.

Concerns about standards

Exams have a reputation for being 'rigorous'; continuous assessment, by contrast, raises the worry that the marks awarded cannot be trusted. It seems to be a system that could easily be abused, by a teacher who is overly generous to their own students, or, perhaps, by a teacher who overly penalizes a student whom they feel has not made best use of the wise advice the teacher has provided.

This worry is misplaced. Teachers take their assessment responsibilities very seriously. They do not want to get it wrong. Most teachers are grateful to receive guidance about how to mark properly: how to interpret assessment criteria and marking grids. They appreciate the exemplar pieces of work and commentaries giving guidance on marking which awarding bodies make available and take seriously the task of matching students' work to the criteria described in the marking grids.

In the United Kingdom, the awarding bodies have a responsibility to establish national standards. This is an extremely rigorous process.

External moderators, who are themselves subject to processes of standardization, inspect a sample of work from each school or college. In the light of this inspection, the awarding bodies have the power either to uphold the marks that teachers have awarded, or to adjust them, to bring them into line with the national standard. As part of this process, reports are produced to inform teachers of how well they have applied the marking grids, and to make recommendations of how they can improve their practice. The work of the awarding bodies is itself the subject of ongoing scrutiny by the government's regulatory body.

It would be naïve to ignore the potential for malpractice in continuously assessed qualifications. But the right answer to this problem is not to reject this educationally valuable form of assessment, but to ensure that a system of rigorous checks of the kind described above is in place to safeguard against malpractice.

Developing an assessment model for philosophical learning

I have been emphasizing the importance of well-designed assessment instruments. If we want to allow students space to think philosophically and enquire more freely and creatively, careful thought needs to go into the design of the criteria by which they will be assessed. Get these right, and you have a qualification in which learning can be liberating as well as academically rigorous. Get them wrong, and what may have been intended as an exciting venture in new ways of teaching and learning can become another sterile hoop-jumping regime. As a case study of a programme in which a great deal of thought went into the question of how to create 'fit-for-purpose' assessment of philosophical learning, we will consider the path followed by the developers of the PoS course.

The development of PoS began thanks to a lunch-time conversation at a science teacher training conference at the University of York, in 1999. I was talking to two colleagues: Becky Parker, a science teacher and, at the time, member of the Education Committee of the Royal Society, and Dr Elizabeth Swinbank from the University of York Science Education Group. We were discussing the problem that, in many lessons, interesting philosophical topics come up, but there simply isn't time to pursue them. Typically, a teacher might allow a few minutes for discussion of these questions. I remarked that it would be nice if there were a qualification in the history and philosophy of science for post-16 year olds. This would mean that all the exciting conversations could be the main point of a lesson, not simply an interesting diversion. So instead of having to call a halt after a few minutes of exciting discussion of a question such as 'What came before the big bang?', 'What is the mind?' or 'Is there such a thing as truth?', these questions could become the main focus around which philosophical learning happens.

There followed a five-year process of qualification development. This was carried out by a team of teachers, authors and academics led by myself and Elizabeth Swinbank. Funding for development work came from the Wellcome Trust, the Royal Society and the former Particle Physics and Astronomy Research Council. Much of the development work focused on the creation of high quality published resources to support both teachers and students (PoS Project Team, 2007a and 2007b).

The PoS programme was designed to encourage a new way of learning – one in which the development of skills, not the didactic teaching of content, was the most important thing, and in which the aim was not to acquire a great deal of subject knowledge but to equip students to research, analyse, argue and master the protocols and conventions of academic writing. Given the enormously engaging nature of the subject matter, as well as its vast range, we wanted to make the most we could out of the opportunity for classroom discussion and debate and enquiry into questions of the student's own choosing.

The PoS course was piloted in just over 30 schools and colleges between 2004 and 2008 as a free standing AS pilot qualification. From 2006, the government decided it would be a good idea for UK students aged 16–19 to have a chance to do individual extended research projects and so developed the Extended Project Qualification. The PoS course was one of the prototypes for this national qualification, which has grown rapidly since its launch in 2008. Now, PoS is used as a programme for project-based learning with students who are working towards the writing of Extended Project dissertations. There are also published student and teacher resources for the Extended Project Qualification that are based on the PoS model (Swinbank and Taylor, 2009a and 2009b).

The PoS programme is unusual in having no prescribed curriculum content. Since the aim is to equip students to think for themselves about science, we wanted to avoid a curriculum design which was structured around a set of authorized 'ideas about science'. The idea that, in philosophy, there is a set of 'authorized' ideas, from which one has to begin, is a problematic one. If philosophy is viewed as a methodology – the method of critical examination of the conceptual clarity of the ideas which we use when thinking – then it is a subject which, by its nature, resists a purely didactic approach. Learning philosophy involves learning to think in a philosophical way, and that happens through activities such as discussion, debate, and trying to write in depth and from your own point of view about a question with a philosophical character. In the development of the PoS course, we wanted students to learn to develop their own philosophical ideas about science, not simply to absorb a prescribed set of philosophical statements.

A radical alternative to a content-driven curriculum would be to jettison content entirely and focus simply on skills development. There are qualifications available to pre-university students, such as 'critical thinking', which are solely concerned with the development of the student's powers of reasoning. Students on such courses learn about valid and invalid forms of argument and how to lay out arguments so as to exhibit their logical structure. The focus is on the skill of argument analysis, and there is no 'content' to be learned, as such.

But students do need something to think about, if they are going to develop their thinking skills. So we cannot jettison content and just teach skills. What we can do – and what makes for a very interesting and challenging exercise in curriculum development – is to work out a matrix of skills, and then choose the best content for the development of those skills. This is the approach we took with the PoS course. Case studies and topics were selected because they provided good contexts for skills development. This means that the teaching programme is not wedded to these materials: if alternative materials will work just as well for the purpose of developing skills, then they can be substituted in. It is for this reason that the model is also potentially highly transferable. The same skill sets can be developed using case studies and topics from entirely different subject fields. This is the avenue down which subsequent development work was to go.

One of the key questions we had to face when we were developing the qualification was 'how will it be assessed?' The key to the design of good assessment tools is contained in that rather ugly phrase: 'fitness for purpose'. We were aiming to develop a qualification in which students began to develop and defend their own philosophical ideas about a scientifically based question of their own choosing. We also wanted them to be able to present their work, both via a well-written academic dissertation and in an oral presentation. We therefore needed to assess how well students could develop appropriate research questions, carry out research, develop a reasoned defence of their own answer to the question and communicate their research findings in writing and orally. In short, we wanted to assess a set of skills: skills in research, analysis of ideas, argumentation and presentation. How were we to assess this?

If we had written a content heavy, Greeks-to-the-Modern-Age (Plato to NATO) course, it would have been natural to have had assessment by examination. There would have been questions about what Aristotle had to say about the four causes, what Karl Popper had to say about the definition of science, and so on. Examinations like these are good for the purpose of testing factual recall. To a lesser extent, they do offer a chance to assess thinking skills too. But given that our main aim was to help students to develop their skills in thinking and research, we wanted this element to be the dominant one in the assessment model.

The most exciting thing about the PoS course was that it provided a chance for teachers to break out of the 'spoon-feeding' regime and a provided a chance for students to think for themselves. We wanted maximum scope for discussion, debate and the critical exploration of a wide range of philosophical points of view. Given the way in which contemporary education is heavily shaped by assessment, we knew that if the final assessment was by means of a written examination, the way in which the course was taught would be squeezed, with the return of the 'teaching-to-the-test' culture which we were so keen to break free from. The exam-based approach was too mechanistic for us. So in the end it was decided that there would not be an exam. Instead, the assessment would be by means of a written dissertation and oral presentation.

The decision to assess by means of a dissertation and presentation was a key decision. It freed up the process of developing the qualification. It also freed things up for students, who now had the opportunity to be truly creative. Although we put in place some parameters, designed to ensure that the questions students chose were academically appropriate and that they were linked to science and philosophy, the scope for free choice of question was huge.

But at the same time, because there was a strong backbone of academic skills which were to be assessed, the work produced by the students was highly rigorous. The assessment criteria for the dissertation relate to research skills, skills in writing and skills in dialectic: thinking for yourself, putting forward an idea and defending it against counter-arguments. To do this with research materials and arguments of an appropriate level, in a sustained manner, over the course of a process which may take more than a year, is anything but a soft option.

Assessing the quality of philosophical projects

The most important feature of any assessment system is that it is 'fit-for-purpose': it needs to do the job of discriminating between better and worse instances of the type of activity being assessed. When it comes to the assessment of philosophy, I have been arguing that much of what we want to assess is best found by inviting students to write extended philosophical dissertations. It is here that the qualities of reflection, critical thinking, precise, careful written expression, and judicious use of research sources to bolster an argument and provide an interesting setting can best be developed. And, if the right assessment criteria are in place, it is these attributes which will be rewarded when the work is marked. Now it happens to be the case that a number of such schemes exist. Qualifications such as the IB Extended Essay, and the Extended Project, the development of which was informed by the work done on the PoS course, do indeed reward these attributes, and hence, provide vehicles for valid assessment of students' developing prowess in philosophical reasoning.

This is not the place for a lengthy exposition of the mechanics of assessment: this information is provided by the awarding bodies and in any case, when it comes to assessment, the devil is in the detail, and the details are different for different qualifications. Here, however, are a few general pointers about how to assess student dissertations which have a distinctively philosophical flavour.

Consider the quality of thought that goes into the choice of the research question

The best projects are those which have a clear, specific, well-focused central objective, which will often be in the form of a question. When assessing this aspect of a dissertation, look for evidence that a student has thought hard about their chosen question. Have they simply picked a question, or have they thought about what it means? Has their chosen question emerged as a result of an iterative process of reflection and improvement? Weaker students will simply state a question, or even fail to include a question at all. More able students will be able to analyse their question. They will be able to identify the philosophical aspects of their question, and explore these to some extent. The strongest students will be able to identify the relevant philosophical aspects of their question with precision and write in detail about these. They will be able to identify and explain the main philosophical frameworks that are relevant to their question. They will also be able to 'locate' their question: they will show how it fits into a wider framework of ideas or historical developments. What is it that motivates the question? What is the rationale behind it? Why does it matter? Weaker students may not have a great deal to say here; middle ability students will usually be able to say something about the meaning and significance of the question. The best dissertations are those in which the student is able to explain the importance of their question – both its general significance and its personal relevance. To write in this way means that the student will have had to 'read around' their question, so in rewarding students who can contextualize their question, we are rewarding the work of attempting to gain a more inclusive, synoptic understanding.

Consider the quality of research in the literature review

We explored the different levels of research skill in Chapter 3. At the lower end, we find students for whom research is mainly a matter of collecting source materials, with little analysis or synthesis. In the mid-range are those students who manage to link sources to some extent and who include some analytical elements. The best literature reviews are written by students who know how to analyse sources, extracting information that is relevant to their dissertation and explaining its meaning. They will also tend to link sources to create a literature review with narrative flow. There will be careful consideration of the reliability of sources (and this will be genuine: it is all well and good for a student to claim that they have corroborated sources, but can they give evidence of this?).

Students should be rewarded for their initiative in the research process. If all the sources used are those which came top of the list produced by a search engine, then the mark awarded for research would usually be lower than that given to a student who has dug deeper and found more unusual material. In most cases, it is a sign of better quality research if a wider range of sources has been used – both a larger number and a variety of types. But there are students who produce high quality research by in-depth examination of a few sources (e.g. if their project is on a literary theme, and they have studied a small number of books or plays closely).

The mark awarded for research should reflect the care with which students have cited their sources. Source citation is an important academic protocol. Even in the weakest projects, there should be a bibliography which indicates the location of the sources that were used. A consistent system of referencing characterizes mid to high mark work, and the best projects have detailed, well-constructed bibliographies and are well referenced throughout. When marking this aspect of a dissertation, vigilance about potential plagiarism is essential. A sudden change in the style of writing (particularly if it suddenly becomes impressively formal), a change of font, inclusion of material which cannot plausibly be produced even by an able teenage student, the surprising use of a well-placed semicolon: these may well indicate that some of the material included is not the student's own. Such indicators invite further investigation.

Consider the quality of argument in the discussion section

The assessment of philosophical argument broadly follows the levels indicated on the 'ladder of logic' described in Chapter 2. When students are writing a philosophical dissertation, they should include arguments. There should be a clearly stated point of view which they support with reasoning based on their research. At the lower end, students struggle to write argumentatively. They tend to describe arguments, rather than actually getting involved in building a case for their own answer to the research question. Students in the middle of the ability range tend to write more discursively: they will talk about the issue and perhaps give some arguments, but this will be patchy. There will not be a developed line of argument running through the entire discussion section. There will probably also be limited consideration of counter-arguments at most. The strongest discussions are those in which there is precise identification of the point of view to be defended. Here, the student may make use of appropriate philosophical terminology. So, for example, they may state that they will be giving a consequentialist defence of the use of animals for medical research. They will go on to give supporting arguments and consider and reply to counter-arguments. In the strongest dissertations, the dialectical structure is strong throughout: the discussion is clearly organized so as to build up the logical case for what the student wants to argue. Counter-arguments will be considered carefully and in some depth; the student will show that they have thought seriously about the viewpoint of those who disagree with what they are arguing.

Consider the quality of writing throughout the dissertation

One of the virtues of well-produced philosophy is that it reads well. The greatest of the great philosophers took care to express themselves in a manner which was not simply clear but also enjoyable to read. Books such as Plato's *Apology*, Descartes' *Meditations* or Hume's *Dialogues Concerning Natural Religion* are simply wonderful to read. Obscurity is not a virtue. Clarity and coherence characterize well-written philosophy.

When thinking about the quality of a student's work, a helpful question to ask is: 'Is the dissertation coherent?' Does it contain, at however low a level, a central idea which the student sustains throughout? The weakest dissertations will border on incoherence, though total incoherence is rare. More commonly, students drift between more and less coherent writing. Projects of middling quality often contain elements of good writing, with some organization, direction and structure, but also sections that are poorly produced: ill-focussed, irrelevant or clumsily expressed. A key element to look for here is the linkage between the various sections of the project. If a student understands their topic well, they will be able to organize their work so that the different sections are clearly linked. It will be clear why they have included the material that they have. A good indicator that a student has not really understood their topic is the inclusion of lots of irrelevant detail, or discontinuities, in which they jump from one idea to another, thus creating the suspicion that they are simply trying to fill the page and have not really thought about what it is that they are writing about.

Strong philosophical dissertations are almost always very well written. They will exhibit the virtues of clear structure, good logical ordering of the various sections, and signposting, in which the writer helps the reader to see where the argument is going. The student will have taken care over their use of terminology, with appropriate but not excessive use of technical philosophical terms. Sentences will be well composed and there should be strong spelling, punctuation and grammar. There will be a sense of balance in the work: the introductory sections will be of a sensible length and the main sections (the literature review and discussion) will be well-developed but not rambling. The writing will also be done using an appropriately formal academic register, with use of the first person only where necessary. Above all, it will be clear what the student is trying to say. It is a sign of significant weakness if you feel that you have had to do the work of constructing the argument from the pieces that the student has presented. I like to push the best students really hard here, getting them to draft and redraft, until the finished product really does make sense and read well.

Consider the quality of self-reflection that has gone into the dissertation writing process

A project is a process, and there should be evidence of ongoing thought about the aims of the dissertation, the research process and the central arguments. This can come through in an activity log which students produce to accompany the dissertation, and it can also come through in a reflective review which they write as part of their evaluation of the project at its conclusion. In both of these elements, less able students tend to write descriptively, and stronger students show evidence of ongoing reflection. The poorest activity logs are, so to speak, wooden: they give details of what has been done, but provide little indication of why the student made the decisions that they did. The strongest students appreciate the idea that a project is a creative journey, one powered by ongoing philosophical reflection. The best activity logs capture some of the key moments on this journey – the points at which they realized that their question was not well formed, or that they had neglected an important area, or that a key argument was invalid.

When it comes to writing an evaluative review of the whole project, it is always impressive when a student is able to put their finger on the weaknesses in the work they have produced. This is not something many students like to do, but it is a healthy sign that they have absorbed the lesson that philosophy is about self-criticism, as well as thinking critically about other people's ideas, and it is something to reward when marking the review section of a dissertation.

The dead hand of Jeremy Bentham

Up until now, we have been exploring what can be done by way of creating space for a more philosophical approach to teaching within the confines of an educational system which is dominated by assessment by means of written examinations. The dominance of assessment is itself a reflection of the pressure which a culture of accountability exerts on education. Practitioners are expected to demonstrate that they can be trusted to do their job by achieving externally set targets. The culture of accountability measures has had a huge, and, arguably, distorting effect on education. It is worth our while considering the philosophical roots of such a system.

If you visit University College London, you can see the dead body of Jeremy Bentham at the end of the South Cloisters of the College's main building. Bentham, one of the founders of the utilitarian theory of ethics, according to which the right course of action is the one which leads to the greatest happiness for the greatest number, decreed in his will that, on his death, his body should be preserved and put on display. According to one story, he is brought out during College Council meetings, where he is recorded as 'present, but not voting' (UCL, 2010).

Bentham equated happiness with pleasure and suggested that not only could pleasure (and the avoidance of pain) be taken to be the goal of all ethical action, but that its elements could be defined with such precision as to make it a measureable quantity. The elements of pleasure were, he said: intensity, duration, certainty, fecundity, propinquity, purity and extent (Bentham, 1781, chapter 4). And the scientific process of assigning positions on the scale of pleasure and pain to different actions was to be done by the use of what he called the 'felicific calculus'.

Benthamite utilitarianism is a scheme to measure the immeasurable. What Bentham wanted to do was to take the quality of goodness (which exists in many different forms), and reduce it to a single measurable quantity (the sum total of pleasure). Bentham is the philosophical founding father of all schemes which seek to reduce qualities to quantities and replace judgements of value with measurements of outcomes. It is his dead hand which extends over all the apparatus of bureaucratic accountability.

The attempt to reduce qualitative judgements to quantifiable measures has had a profound and distorting effect on education. 'Results' become the means by which students, teachers and whole schools are judged. The resulting pressure to achieve results creates an educational culture in which teaching-to-the-test takes the place of learning for its own sake.

Good education contains many aspects which cannot be measured. But such is the influence of the utilitarian approach that, instead of this fact being used to put outcome measures into context, we end up allowing the system of measurement to determine the way in which we teach. A consequence of the emphasis on measurable outcomes is that less tangible qualities – like depth of understanding, ethical awareness and creativity – come to be taken less seriously than things that seem easier to measure (like, for instance, accuracy of factual recall). One of the things which a Benthamite system squeezes out, ironically, is philosophy. There isn't a great deal of time for stepping back and thinking about what it all means when everyone is preoccupied by the need to achieve results.

Understanding undervalued

A philosophical approach to teaching gives pride of place to understanding. To be philosophical is to find things puzzling – to take ideas which ordinarily pass unexamined and probe their perplexing aspects. The goal of this enterprise is not to raise a general sense of confusion, but to enable a clearer appreciation of the meaning of things and awareness of the limits of knowledge. Philosophy's contribution to knowledge lies in its contribution to understanding.

When I trained to teach, the National Curriculum was just being launched – replete with more than 100 attainment targets. When training as a science teacher, I learned a little about why it is that students find scientific understanding so very difficult. One reason for this is that they do not come to their science lessons cold: from a very young age, they have been observing the world and enquiring about how it works. They will have ideas of their own about topics such as electricity. Before they can understand the world scientifically, then, I was taught that it is necessary to tease out these preconceptions and subject them to critical challenge. We were trained to create schemes of work which reflected this 'constructivist' approach.

I quickly learned on teaching practice that most of this enlightened approach would have to be thrown out of the window. There simply wasn't time. You might have a single lesson in which to teach about series circuits, before you were on to the next attainment target. What mattered was ensuring that all the targets had been 'delivered'. Understanding was a luxury that time-poor teachers and students could not really afford.

If we want students to enquire, and to begin to understand, we need to allow them time to question. Thankfully, ever since its introduction, successive reforms of the National Curriculum have slimmed down the amount of prescribed content. Recent trends also suggest that the amount of examined assessment which students have to endure may be set to fall. There have been curriculum innovations, such as the introduction of project qualifications, in which there is no prescribed content at all. There has also been discussion about a reduction in the number of opportunities for resitting modules. All of this suggests that the pendulum is beginning to swing back towards a place where the teacher will have more scope to explore ideas in depth and help students to begin understanding them more fully. From the point of view of those of us who advocate a more philosophical approach, this is good news. It suggests that we really can think seriously about how best to organize our teaching so as to promote a deeper level of understanding.

Time to think

Understanding involves thinking not just about items of knowledge on their own, but about how one piece of knowledge is linked to others. To understand is to perceive connections. It helps students to understand what they are learning if they have some sense of how knowledge emerged historically. It also helps if they are able to think philosophically about what they are learning: if they have been encouraged to learn through critical questioning, rather than just soaking up information.

Consider scientific education. Many students really struggle to understand science. This is unsurprising, when we reflect on the abstract way in which much science is still taught. Although there have been attempts in recent years to introduce elements of 'how science works' or 'ideas and evidence' into science teaching, it remains the case that most of what students learn in science lessons is taught in a way which divorces scientific knowledge from the social, historical and philosophical context in which it was derived. This is an educational failing and a missed opportunity. It is a missed opportunity because bringing the human element into our teaching makes it more interesting. The story of the development of our understanding of the world is full of dramatic episodes with which to enliven teaching and move it away from a sterile recitation of facts to be learned for the next test.

This point was made in an anecdote told by Cambridge Professor of Philosophy, Simon Blackburn:

> When she was in her teens, my daughter came home from her school – one of the country's best High Schools for girls – and announced that she was through with science. I said that was a pity, and asked why. It turned out that they had been 'learning the pendulum', and this consisted, apparently, in solving for velocity at the bottom of the swing using the equation of potential energy at the top and kinetic energy at the bottom. I asked what the problem was, and she said she didn't understand what this thing

'energy' was, that was the same throughout: there was nothing she could see that stayed the same about the bob at the top and bottom of its swing. I asked if she had put her problem to the teacher. Yes. And what did she say? 'Get on and solve the equation'. (Blackburn, 2010, p. 25)

As Simon Blackburn explains, the problem here is that students may end up 'understanding' what they need to do to pass their exams, but they lack a proper understanding of the concepts that are used in what they are learning. But to gain understanding, a step is required which takes us beyond simply 'learning' and even 'knowing'. It is a step that requires learning to see the knowledge one has gained as a whole, being able to appreciate how it can be put to use, and being able to 'internalize' it: to see it for oneself. This step can only be taken by students who are actively thinking for themselves about what they are being taught.

The journey sketched here is the one to which Professor A. C. Grayling refers, when he speaks of the progression from the acquisition of data, to knowledge and thence to *understanding*:

[K]nowledge as such is not yet the point of an education, though certainly it is a central part of it. The stage beyond knowledge is understanding – and this is the stage that really counts. Understanding what you know is what makes it genuinely usable. It stands at the level of insight and effectiveness. It is as far beyond knowledge as knowledge is beyond mere data. To turn data into knowledge, the data have to be ordered and arranged; to understand what one knows, one has to have worked with the knowledge, applied it, tested it in the practice of reasoning and debate. To produce the sort of person who has such understanding is the goal of education. (Grayling, 2010, pp. 10–11)

The danger of a content-heavy curriculum is that it leads to an educational system which produces students who have a head full of data but nevertheless lack knowledge and, most crucially, simply *do not understand* what they have been taught. True understanding involves the capacity to apply knowledge – to put it to use, in defending ideas and in deriving further knowledge. It has to do with the making of links; with seeing the bigger picture; with recognizing how one set of ideas is logically related to others. All this takes time, and, in the sense that we have been using it, the application of some philosophical reflection.

Where, in a crowded curriculum, is there to be found the space for the reflective, focused, perceptive thought which allows the mind to gain an appreciation not just for the fact that the jigsaw pieces do all link, but that they link to make a picture, which is to be appreciated in its own right? Space does exist, but it is hard not to feel that education would be in better shape if we pushed the boundaries back a little at this point. There needs to be some pruning, in the name of liberal learning, of the assessment regime. There is no call for the elimination of examined assessment. But reduction in the frequency of testing, in the number of modules which a subject comprises and in the opportunity for tests to be re-sat, together with some creative thinking about how there could be more assessment of general education and the all-important capacity for synoptic understanding: these would be steps well worth taking.

If we didn't have such detailed specifications, such prescriptive mark schemes, so very many examinations, such mechanical accountability measures, such an obsession with quantity rather than quality and such directive measures for what and how we should teach – if education gave a little more space for us to simply enjoy teaching and learning – then it would be that bit easier to get students excited again about the love of learning, and to share with them the ideas which make some of us passionate enough to choose to spend our lives teaching.

This, then, is a direction in which we should be looking to go. But let me end on an optimistic note. We can start down this road. The space exists, if we look for it, for the sort of richer, deeper, more liberating, more philo-sophically inspiring and empowering education that we have been describing. There already exist qualifications which have been designed specifically to open up such space and they are achieving their purpose. Here is how one teacher described his experience of teaching on one such course:

> I am really enthusiastic about the course. I think it's prob-
> ably the most enjoyable teaching I've ever done in my
> whole teaching career. I think it's because for once the stu-
> dents and I are actually exploring knowledge, for the love
> of exploring knowledge, rather than trying to prove that
> Ohm's Law is still Ohm's Law. (PoS pilot teacher, quoted in
> Levinson et al., 2008, p. 29)

Philosophically Speaking: The Future

A School of Thought

It is time to reflect, in the light of what we have explored, on how we can bring about an integration of a philosophical approach on a school-wide basis. The question is: how can we turn our schools into 'Schools of Thought'? This is a question about a whole-school ethos. It means giving consideration to all aspects of school life – not just the content of the curriculum, but also the way in which teaching and learning happen. It involves thinking about the ways in which we assess, how we understand ourselves as educators and the way in which we relate to students, in both formal and informal contexts. It means thinking too about the nature of philosophy, and about our own area of subject expertise, and how these are related. It means, in effect, applying philosophy both within our educational practice and to that practice itself: stepping back a little, and asking some of those deep questions, about why we do it, and what we hope education can achieve.

My suggestion is that philosophy can become a significant part of a school's ethos. Seeing things in this light suggests the exciting potential that philosophy has, to make a difference at a school-wide level. It indicates too the scope of the challenge. It involves thinking about all the elements that go into shaping the sort of education a school aims to provide. Developing a philosophical ethos is not something which happens overnight. It is something which emerges as a result of deliberate planning. It calls for commitment from school leaders, who have to share the vision for this sort of education.

I am going to describe some ingredients that, put together, help to create an atmosphere in which philosophical reflection becomes part and parcel of the life of the school. Figure 7.1 provides a conceptual map of some of the elements which can help to shape a school-wide philosophical ethos. They are not essentials: they are ideas which have been tried and found useful. You may well look at these and feel you can think of better alternative steps to take. There are many roads which lead to philosophy, and it would be a travesty of the subject for anyone to suggest that theirs is the One True Way.

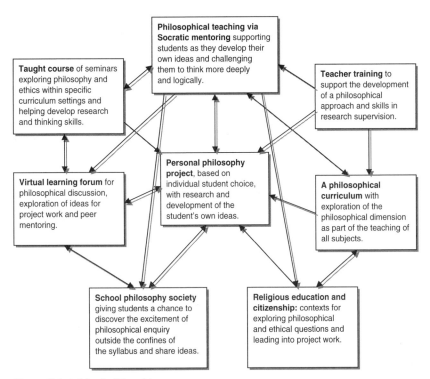

Figure 7.1 A School of Thought

A personal philosophy project

We have discussed the value of project work as a vehicle for philosophical exploration. What I want to draw attention to here is the centrality of project work as a component in forming a School of Thought. A School of Thought is characterized by free discussion of ideas about the things that matter: this will take place both within lessons and outside of the curriculum. A personal philosophy project is a place where students can choose to explore some of these ideas – the ones which really resonate with them – in greater depth. It is also a place where they can begin to explore 'outside the box': crossing curriculum boundaries and thinking about a topic in a way which brings together knowledge they have gained from their own research and from their studies in other subjects. Each of these elements – personal engagement with ideas, deeper thinking and a wider, cross-curricular perspective are at the heart of a philosophical approach to learning, and are at the centre of the ethos of a School of Thought.

The personal philosophy project is a place where philosophical learning finds its fullest expression. The philosophical work that students put into these projects in turn becomes a resource for other elements of the life of the school. One of the most rewarding features of project work is that it allows the student to 'own' the ideas which they develop. They often learn more about their chosen topic than their teachers know, and are enthusiastic enough to want to share this with others. They may be asked to speak about their work in a lesson the theme of which coincides with their area of research. Or they could speak in a school assembly, or to a group of younger students. Or they could present their research in a philosophy society meeting or at another extracurricular society. In these ways, the deep exploration of philosophical ideas which project work makes possible can enrich other elements of the school's intellectual life.

Philosophical teaching via Socratic mentoring

Socratic mentoring by philosophically inclined teachers is the driving force behind a School of Thought. We have explored in detail the techniques which go into this way of working with students. It is worth reflecting too on the arena within which this critical yet supportive form of engagement with students can find expression. As well as guiding philosophical discussions as part of the taught course preparation for project work and acting as a facilitator to students who are writing their dissertations, Socratic mentors will be using their skills as part of normal classroom teaching and in informal settings outside the classroom.

In a school where the philosophical dimension is valued as a rich and deep part of education, teachers feel increasingly confident to explore philosophical ideas as part of their day-to-day teaching. Socratic mentors begin to develop a 'nose' for philosophy. They sense when something that is said in a lesson is philosophically interesting, and learn to ask a question which causes everyone else in the group to stop and turn their attention to the matter.

To a philosopher, there is nothing commonplace about the world around us, and this is one reason why it is such an effective subject for stimulating students to begin thinking. Ask a question such as 'Are you sure that the table in front of you is real?', or 'The colour of those flowers – do you think it exists in the flower, or is it in your mind?' and you have stepped straight into the world of philosophical mystery. The Socratic mentor is a teacher who has learned to ask questions like these, even though they may not feel that they have very satisfactory answers. They do not know what 'learning outcome' the discussion will reach – but they do know that something important will happen once students start to think seriously about such questions, the fruits of which sometimes only show themselves much later. To teach philosophically is to be unafraid to take a class of students into the strange and confusing world of philosophy. To a teacher who is willing to experiment in this way, opportunities will present themselves no matter what the topic of the lesson is. They will constantly be on the lookout for opportunities to spark off philosophical discussion when talking to students outside the classroom as well. The quizzical, restless, probing, questioning, challenging activity of the Socratic mentor is the lifeblood of a School of Thought.

The taught course

We saw in Chapter 3 that the taught course component of a project-based philosophy programme is the platform from which successful philosophical project work is launched. One feature of good projects is that they go beyond the confines of a single discipline. It may be that this happens by exploring the philosophical depths of a question that has come up within a subject context. Or, more commonly, students may choose a question which can fruitfully be studied from a range of different subject perspectives. I have already described the PoS course, in which the history, philosophy and ethics of science are combined. At the school where I teach, similar programmes have been created, bringing together disciplines such as philosophy, English, history and classics, or politics, economics and business studies. This is an approach which other schools and colleges have been using too.

The idea here is to link 'cognate' disciplines: groups of subjects which fit alongside each other and offer different perspectives which can be applied to whatever research question the student chooses. These cross-curricular taught courses are taught by specialists from each of these disciplines, who each run seminars in which philosophical and ethical questions from their area of expertise are explored.

Programmes such as these are valuable in helping to show that many of the most interesting questions are best explored from the stand-point of more than one discipline. But they have a wider value too. The opportunity to design a taught course which will serve as a basis for project work is, in effect, an invitation to teachers to write their own mini-curriculum. There are some constraints: the course needs to prepare students for project work, and so skills such as research and critical thinking need to be developed. The course should not be overfull of 'content', but should instead focus on case-study discussion of material which will stimulate ideas for potential projects. But these constraints leave a great deal of freedom for the teacher to innovate and improvise. Here, then, is a chance to teach freely, without the constant need to check whether the ideas you are exploring are 'on the syllabus'. To a large extent, you write the syllabus. In my experience, teachers who are just longing to find greater freedom from the constraints of examined courses leap at the chance to get involved in this sort of teaching. The taught course is a tonic. I have seen teachers rejuvenated by having the chance to get involved in project-based teaching. As ripples of enthusiasm spread out to the rest of the school, the benefits are felt widely.

Entering the Philosophy Zone

Philosophical discussion and virtual learning go together very well indeed. Students are at home in the world of social networking and can contribute ideas fluently and eloquently. I find that asking students to post their thoughts in a discussion thread following an initial stimulus can yield excellent results. It is a form of written expression that retains the benefits of real-time interactivity. If students are asked to write a short essay, then they may well compose their thoughts more carefully than they would if expressing them as part of a group discussion. However, they will not get immediate feedback. Essay writing is not interactive. Conversely, in a group discussion, there is opportunity for interaction and the interplay of argument and counter-argument, but the contributions will not benefit from the same degree of forethought as could go into a written response.

Online discussion lets you get the best of both worlds. With postings to a discussion page on a virtual learning forum, there is the chance for interaction, as one student responds to the posting of another. But there is also the chance for students to take a little time to compose their thoughts. In fact, the medium creates some pressure for them to do so: the fact that what they write will be stored in the thread and be visible to everyone who logs on makes most students think a little more carefully before they express themselves (though equally, it creates an opportunity for the joker in the class to try their hand at subversion, a fact which implies the need for moderation of discussions).

I have found that using a discussion forum provides an excellent alternative to face-to-face seminars during the taught course component of a project-based philosophy programme. I find that there are two distinct purposes for which virtual learning can be useful:

- Discussion of philosophical stimulus material, at an early stage in the programme, as a way of developing skills and suggesting project ideas. For these discussions, the stimulus is usually chosen by the teacher.
- Peer-mentoring and sharing of ideas about potential projects. Many students find it helpful to post a question (e.g. 'I am thinking of doing a project about the environment. Any ideas?').

As with face-to-face discussions, the key to a really good online discussion is finding the right stimulus. The same rules apply here as apply to classroom discussions: choose a question which will interest students, which some of them will have opinions about and which is controversial (see Chapter 2, 'Questions of interest').

When I was first experimenting with online philosophical discussion, I recorded short podcasts with my colleague, Emma Williams, the philosopher-in-residence at the school where I teach. These podcasts were designed to provide some of the 'opening moves' in a philosophical debate. We kept things brief, and deliberately open-ended, offering an initial exploration of some of the main arguments on the topic, but avoiding giving any answers. These podcasts worked well, but it quickly became clear to us that there is already a treasure trove of really good philosophical material – short, punchy podcasts, controversial clips from unusual speakers, lectures by world-famous academics, excerpts from debates between religious apologists and sceptics and stimulating articles from dedicated philosophy websites – freely available on the internet. So now, we will often simply select a good short (5–10 mins max.) clip from a web resource, create a thread, and let the discussion get going.

I am sometimes asked about how we manage to get students to post to the discussions. The answer is that we run them more or less exactly as we would run a face-to-face discussion – except that group interacts online. That is to say, students will sometimes be in the same room, or in adjacent rooms, and be expected to participate in the online discussion just as they would in group discussion during a lesson. This may seem a strange arrangement. Why not just talk to each other? There are, however, a number of things which happen during online interaction which make it rather different, and worth doing, even if the group could actually discuss without the benefit of the online platform. One of these benefits, as already noted, is that they tend to compose their responses more thoughtfully and carefully. Another is that the thread remains in place, so that others can pick it up later in the week. Many students will spend time reading what has been written before they decide what to add and so learn from each other. A further benefit is that students start to behave differently once they are writing their thoughts, instead of speaking. There are some who prefer to express themselves this way. The more nervous members of the group sometimes 'team up' and write joint postings. Students – 'digital natives' – will often trawl the web to find links or supporting data for their arguments, and bring these into the discussion. Finally, if the core discussion is happening in one place with a group of students logged in simultaneously, there is the possibility of remote users logging on and joining an active discussion. This happened in quite striking fashion during a student conference, in which I arranged for around 100 students to join an online philosophical discussion forum simultaneously. They were situated in computer rooms all within a few hundred metres of each other – and were joined in real time by two students from Australia.

I must admit that I had hoped that the online Philosophy Zone would become a place of vibrant philosophical discussion that would happen spontaneously and continue outside of lessons. On one occasion, I have seen this happen, with a small group of extremely dedicated students. But for the most part, I find that students are no more likely to join an online philosophy discussion hosted by their teacher outside of lesson time, than they would be to spontaneously gather on the street corner and begin philosophizing. It is easy to think that because they chat naturally enough on social networking sites, the same will happen if you set up a philosophy forum. But I suspect that the level of spontaneous interaction varies inversely with the depth of philosophical focus. It takes careful stage-setting to get a really good philosophical discussion going in the classroom and the discussion needs facilitation. The same is true online.

To round out this section, I have included an excerpt from one of the Philosophy Zone discussions. Here, a group of 16–17-year-old students, who have been following the PoS programme, have been invited to discuss a philosophical question about the origins of the universe. Points to note here include the extent to which the responses are composed. They tend to be more carefully worded and structured than the things that would be said in a face-to-face seminar. You will notice too that I play an active role as the Socratic mentor, intervening to help focus the discussion a little, and get some argument/counter-argument going. I chose to intervene towards the end of this thread. If you are the teacher-facilitator, it is best to be cautious about posting. You need to be reasonably confident that the student you engage in argument won't mind 'taking the teacher on'. This tends to be something which only the more confident of the group feel comfortable in doing.

The other thing to notice here is that students don't mind having a little fun, and that is all to the good. I sometimes describe philosophy as a 'fundamental activity'. It begins with fun and ends with mental activity. Here, you can see both:

The Big Bang Theory   by John Taylor
Do you think that the big bang theory supports the idea of a creator God, or disproves it, or is it simply irrelevant?

Re: The Big Bang Theory   by Bisman
I think that the big bang theory helps support the idea of a God, because something had to set off the big bang, and while scientists may find a cause of the big bang, something will have had to set that off as well, so no matter how far back you look, there has to be a beginning and, therefore, I think that science helps support the idea that God started something, and the universe was created from it.

Re: The Big Bang Theory   by Catriona
I think it is irrelevant, as God does not exist and there is no factual evidence whatsoever to prove God. Yes, many people believe in a God but that is no reason to take God into account as the creator of the universe. Some people have religions that have aliens and even jedi as their gods. So surely if God could have created the universe, so could a green blobby man and Obi Wan Kenobi?

Re: The Big Bang Theory   by Polly
Aliens don't just have to be green and blobby – they are just foreign beings – and there is much more chance of life existing on other planets than there is a supernatural being in the sky. I just don't feel anyone yet can come to a conclusion, scientific or religious, that explains the origins of the universe.

Re: The Big Bang Theory   by Jinseog
To make use of wordplay, the fact that the big bang theory is a theory means that it can't really prove or disprove anything on its own. But I think that at least while we don't possess full knowledge, it's what we believe that counts. Christians may never really know that God exists, but they have seen and experienced enough to believe so. In a very similar fashion, big bang theorists have seen enough evidence to believe (but not know) that the big bang theory holds much credibility.

Re: The Big Bang Theory   by John Taylor
Jin – very good point about the theoretical nature of the big bang model. I wonder what you think about Bertrand Russell's argument: If everything has to have a cause, God has a cause; if things can exist without a cause, there is no need for the universe to have a cause – it could just exist?

Re: The Big Bang Theory   by Jinseog
I think it's to do with divine power, for want of a better phrase. As soon as we quantify and understand something, we limit it. It often requires some sort of pentecostal experience to realize the inexplicable and awesome nature of God, so this explanation will doubtless not be enough for most people. But the whole point of God is that he is boundless, and therefore we cannot give him a cause.

Re: The Big Bang Theory   by John Taylor
So the difference is that God is boundless but the universe isn't? What though if the universe turns out to be boundless? Maybe for instance what we call the big bang is only the beginning of our phase in the universe. Perhaps it has always been there.

Philosophical enrichment

One of the merits of a model in which philosophy is woven into the curriculum, rather than simply being taught as a discrete subject, is that it can enrich subjects that are already being taught. Subjects in which students are invited to think about ideas of a philosophical or ethical nature already exist in most schools. Two of the most obvious areas are religious education and citizenship lessons. A programme of PSHE might also afford an opening, if it is used as a forum for discussion of life's deeper questions.

The benefit here is that a philosophical approach can help to make the learning experience more rewarding, by encouraging students to enquire, to reason, argue and discuss, instead of simply having to work through a didactic programme of factual learning. Religious education, in particular, *ought* to be taught using a philosophical approach: this is the proper way to do justice to the open nature of the questions which are raised there. It is a travesty to turn a subject which concerns the deepest questions of all into a game of rote-learning 'standard' responses to exam questions. Religious education ought to be a subject in which students learn to use reason to negotiate some of the deepest, most sensitive, and, at times, inflammatory of questions.

I described in Chapter 2 how a programme of citizenship education can be brought alive by means of a philosophical approach. At its heart, citizenship education is an Aristotelian enterprise: it is about the formation of the intellectual and moral virtues that are required of a good citizen: ethical awareness, a capacity to apply reason to the contentious issues of the day, curiosity about the world and an awareness of the plurality of approaches which people bring to their ethical and political thinking, with a consequent appreciation of the importance of seeing issues from more than one point of view. A course in which basic philosophical and ethical ideas are introduced, followed by a personal philosophical project, is something that I have argued ought to be a part of the education of all pre-16 students. A school's programme of citizenship education is an obvious place for project-based philosophical learning.

My point here is that these are steps which schools can take already. There is no need to await a curriculum reform in which it becomes mandatory: simply take your existing citizenship and religious education programmes and do a 'philosophical audit' on them.

Doing a philosophical audit of a subject

A philosophical audit is a process in which you examine the scheme of work of a subject which *could* be taught in a philosophical, Socratic way, but is currently being taught didactically. So, for instance, you might ask the staff team responsible for citizenship education to see what could be done to weave philosophical and ethical elements through the programme. Here are some suggestions:

- look for the openings for discussion and debate
- ensure that the lessons are structured in a way which encourages the development of skills in argument and independent learning

- strip out any heavily didactic elements (if the students have learned to learn for themselves, they will know how to get their hands on the information in any case)
- use case studies in the early phase of the programme which students can enjoy discussing and through which they can develop their skills in research and critical thinking
- include a personal philosophy project as the main learning outcome.

A philosophical framework for religious education

We noted in Chapter 1 that religious education is an obvious area of the curriculum where a philosophical approach could, and should, find expression. We noted as well that this opportunity is not being made use of as much as it could be. When OFSTED published their report into the strengths and weaknesses of religious education, they expressed concern about 'a limited use of higher-order thinking skills to promote greater challenge'. They also noted that the most effective religious education 'used a range of enquiry skills such as investigation, interpretation, analysis, evaluation and reflection' (OFSTED, 2010, p. 6). This sounds very much like an endorsement of a philosophical approach to the subject.

A philosophical framework can help with the teaching of religious education. A traditional approach to the subject would be to teach it dogmatically: to use it as a means of indoctrination. In recent times, the emphasis has been on teaching about religions, rather than on instructing young people to believe a particular faith. A descriptive approach is encouraged, in which the teachings and traditions of different religions are explained and compared to each other. But teaching religion comparatively can easily lead students to a relativist conclusion: that there is no such thing as truth, but only a plurality of views, each of which is 'true-for-the-believer'.

The problem with both a dogmatic and a relativist approach is that neither of them does anything to encourage critical reflection or discussion. Since it is through discussion that students begin to develop their capacity for independent thought, any block to discussion is a block to intellectual development. This might explain the observations made in the OFSTED report about the limited use of higher-order thinking skills in religious education.

If the dogmatic route is taken, there is simply no point to discussion – at least, not serious discussion. There could be 'discussion' of the sort I described in Chapter 2: the 'let's pretend' type of discussion I might have in a physics lesson, where I know the answers but use the pretence of not knowing as a teaching tool. In a similar manner, for a teacher who 'knows' the truth about religion, any 'conversation' in the class will simply be a device for helping the class come to appreciate 'the truth'. This is the very antithesis of an approach which seeks to help students to think for themselves. It is unlikely to be a very effective pedagogical device, since the students themselves can readily access information about the enormous number, and contradictory nature, of dogmatically reinforced belief systems. They will, therefore, rightly expect that their teacher gives an answer to the question of why they should believe what he is teaching them. And they will also rightly expect more from their teacher than to be told to 'believe because I tell you'.

Concerned to avoid the perils of dogmatism, a teacher might decide that it is better not to think about 'truth' as such. Better, it might be thought, to talk about 'Christian truth', or 'Buddhist truth': to adopt a relativized notion of truth. This approach will appeal to those who wish to respect all systems of belief equally. To the relativist, different systems of belief each have their own validity for the believer. There is, strictly speaking, then, no real disagreement between adherents of different faiths. There is nothing for them to disagree about. They each have their own truth.

But a teacher inclined towards relativism needs to be careful that their eagerness to avoid dogmatism does not lead them into a different pitfall. On the face of it, nothing could be clearer but that there is disagreement about matters of belief, and so the question of where, among the many competing claims, the truth might lie is a reasonable one to ask.

A relativist approach, while on the face of it seeming to respect all religions, may in fact end up *dis*respecting them all. Relativism is a plausible theory about matters of taste. There is no such thing as the truth about the best flavour of ice-cream. This is a domain in which we are simply describing personal preferences. It seems rather demeaning to religion to take this as our model for interpreting religious claims. It implies a radical subjectivity, which does not fit with the way in which religions have, for the most part, understood their own claims. So the claim by the relativist to be showing respect is questionable.

Is there an alternative to the dogmatic and the relativist approaches to religious education? I think that there is: it is the philosophical approach described in this book. We should take the claims of religion seriously, as claims which are advanced as part of the attempt to explain the nature of reality. Like other philosophical claims, they can be subject to critical, reflective examination. We can enquire after their conceptual clarity and the strength of evidence that can be adduced in their favour. We can, in short, approach religious education philosophically, and evaluate it after the fashion described throughout this book.

The great merit of taking this approach is that it encourages the serious discussion of religious belief in the classroom. Instead of foreclosing discussion, either by dogmatically asserting the truth of one particular position, or by dissolving the idea of truth into a relativistic mush, a philosophical approach takes seriously the fact that we do hold to different beliefs in this area, and that it is perfectly reasonable to enquire after the reasons for or against these beliefs.

There is nothing disrespectful about this. Treating someone's beliefs as worth discussion is a way of showing respect. Moreover, we began our account of the character of philosophical discussion by noting that it engenders humility. It proceeds from a recognition of the difficulty of establishing knowledge when it comes to fundamental matters and encourages the virtue of learning from those who hold opposing views.

As an example of the value of approaching religious education within a philosophical context, consider the heated arguments that break out, periodically, about the teaching of creationism in schools. Any suggestion that creationism should be taught as a part of a science lesson is seen as immensely controversial. It is often suggested that it should be taught in religious education instead. But then there is a risk that the science may be misrepresented. Consider, for example, the following Religious Education examination question from 2009:

'The Big Bang theory is no more believable than Creationism.'
Discuss

When this is followed by a mark scheme which allows that candidates are 'free to argue either side of this debate' (OCR, 2009, p. 7), we cannot avoid the feeling that moving the issue into the domain of religious education has not solved the problem.

There is an obvious place for such a discussion, and this is as part of a programme in the history and philosophy of science. Creationism provides as an excellent case study for discussing the nature and limits of scientific explanation, and the criteria by which science and pseudoscience may be demarcated.

Julian Baggini noted the value of a philosophical approach to this contentious issue, and commended the 'measured, intelligent way' that the question of the science/religion relationship is handled in programmes such as PoS (Baggini, 2009). The key is the involvement of philosophy. In place of the dead ends of dogmatism and relativism, religious education has much to gain from the sensitive and intelligent application of a philosophical approach.

Models for running school philosophy societies

The intellectual life of a School of Thought will depend not simply on what is happening within the classroom, but on the richness of its extra-curricular provision. I appreciate that running extracurricular activities can be difficult in schools where resources are tight and teachers are stretched. But if, through after-school or lunch-time slots, it is possible to meet even for a short time with students to continue philosophical discussion in a less formal setting, the rewards will be considerable.

One way of doing this is to run a school philosophy society. Philosophy societies are places where the enthusiasm of the keenest students can find full expression. There will be some students for whom philosophy is 'their thing' – and they will be very keen indeed to keep talking about it. I once ran a group which met on a Thursday evening (I teach in a boarding school). Each week, we would discuss a thought experiment from Julian Baggini's book *The Pig That Wants to be Eaten and Ninety-Nine Other Thought Experiments* (Baggini, 2005). They really enjoyed these sessions: all I had to do was to make sure the discussion didn't get out of hand, such was the level of excitement. Members of the group took it in turn to introduce a new thought experiment each week. Towards the end of the term, as their GCSE mocks approached, they asked if we could keep meeting. I pointed out that they needed to focus on their exams at this stage of the term but suggested that we could continue the discussion by means of an email group, which I offered to set up for them. The next day, I found that they had already started the discussion, which by the time I joined it had over 70 postings. More were added during the course of the day.

Having a core group of devotees is a tremendous asset. It helps other students, who are intrigued, but not (yet) fanatical about philosophy to feel that it is OK to join in. In the case of the group I have just mentioned, younger students started to come too. Many of these students went on to write personal philosophical projects once they were in the sixth form, which helped them a lot with the process of making university applications.

One model, then, for a philosophy society, is a 'student-led' forum for discussion. At the other end of the spectrum, I would also advocate organizing termly philosophy lectures, which can be open to all students. There are many philosophers who are happy to speak to school-age audiences. If you know any academics yourself, it is well worth getting in touch; even if they can't help, they may well know others who can. But care needs to be taken over who is invited. There is a big difference between talking to an audience of 14–18 year olds and lecturing to undergraduates. Not all academics are comfortable with the necessary simplification. I prefer to invite only those whom I know will understand the level that is appropriate to secondary school students.

When you are inviting the speaker, it is important to brief them carefully. The obvious model is for an initial talk of up to 30 minutes, followed by question and answer. The best sessions, though, are those in which the speaker invites the audience to join them on a journey of philosophical enquiry. Philosophers who have the skill and enthusiasm for a Socratic approach can create truly electrifying sessions, in which the students are drawn into a process of thinking through a question along with the speaker. These sessions become opportunities for students to begin getting a feel for the metaphysical mountains of the subject: the big, deep, challenging questions which constitute the very heart of philosophy. You get the feeling of ascending into the philosophical heights, in the company of a skilled guide.

Sessions like these are educationally significant at many levels. There is a danger that, if most of your philosophical education is being done through open discussion in the classroom, students will get the (false) impression that philosophy is an easy-going subject, in which anyone's ideas are more or less as good as anyone else's, and all that is needed is to be fairly eloquent in putting forward your point of view. One of the great merits of inviting in a professional philosopher to give a talk is that students will begin to get a feeling for just how challenging philosophy can be. So although, when briefing speakers, I do emphasize that they should make what they are saying accessible to the students, I also don't mind at all if the students come away from the sessions saying 'Wow – that really made me think.' And they often do.

Philosophical talks have another virtue, which is connected to the theme of this chapter. They are an excellent environment for cross-curricular learning. A talk on a question such as 'Is beauty in the eye of the beholder?' will have something for everyone. Science students will be able to think about the idea of objectivity and whether scientific knowledge is objective in a way that our judgements of beauty are not. Art students will be able to think about the nature of art itself: when we create artworks, are we expressing something personal, or are we try-ing to capture a quality – beauty – which exists independently of us? Historians and students of English will be able to reflect on how ideals of beauty have varied over the years, and whether the idea that one work of art, or novel, is better than another can be defended.

A really good philosophical talk will draw students into the discussion. It offers a chance for them to contribute their own questions and ideas based on what they have been learning in the classroom. Afterwards, they will return to their lessons with new ideas – as well as enthusiasm. One of the reasons why I recommend these extracurricular talks is because of the 'buzz' they create. It is hard work – but you will reap the benefits of increased excitement, as well as a higher profile for philosophical thinking within your school. These sessions have an intangible but very real contribution to make in cultivating a school-wide ethos of philosophical reflection.

We have looked at two models for philosophy society sessions: a stu-dent-led discussion forum and a guest lecture followed by discussion.

Both of these are 'open access': anyone is welcome, though it is wise to target particular year groups, to ensure that the level of discussion is appropriate to the audience. I have a third model for extracurricular, informal philosophical discussion, which is purposefully not open to all. Along with the Head Master of the school where I teach, I run a group for 16–18-year-old students, which is by invitation only and, in a sense, unashamedly elitist. The group, numbering some 20 students, is enigmatically known as the 'Black Lamp Society' and meets once a term. Those invited are selected because they are judged to have something to offer to the discussion and to be best able to profit from being part of the group. The meetings are not advertised widely, although word does get out, and serious applicants are added to the membership list. The group has a student Secretary, appointed by the Head Master, whose job it is to help identify potential new members and to assist in setting up the discussions. The theme for the discussion is a question with an historical and/or philosophical dimension. Current affairs issues are occasionally addressed, but we try to steer away from the merely sensational, and go for questions with real depth.

For each discussion, a short paper is chosen. This will often be an opinion editorial from a quality newspaper, or perhaps a website posting by an academic philosopher or historian. Students are expected to have read the paper beforehand, and for each discussion, one student is invited to introduce the paper and to help chair the discussion. The atmosphere is formal and, I suppose, a little forbidding. We meet in the evening in a large drawing room next to the Head Master's office. Students are expected to be in school uniform and sit in a large circle. After a brief introduction from the Head Master, minutes from previous meetings are read, then the discussion begins. Usually there are two or three staff members present. The expectation is that students will, to borrow an appropriate metaphor, pick up the ball and run with it. This is not a conversation in which the staff expect to have to intervene regularly: it is a chance for some really high-level discussion by bright, well-informed students. And the level of the discussion is often very high indeed.

This is an approach which some have questioned. Is it fair to hand-pick students for such an experience? What about the rest of the school? It might sound unpleasantly exclusive and unhelpfully elitist.

But compare this approach with the way a school might run training for a programme of physical education (PE). Here, while there might be PE training which all can take part in, there will also be sessions in which the focus is on training the best – the strongest athletes, the best tennis players – and no-one is going to complain that these sessions are 'elitist' and not open to all. We accept that, sometimes, it is necessary to work with the best, for their own sake, and for the sake of developing excellence in these areas. And that, in a nutshell, is the reason why, as well as offering Philosophy Society sessions that are open to anyone who wants to come, I think it is worth having some meetings which are just for those who have been identified as, bluntly, potential intellectuals, and who need to be fostered and nurtured, and encouraged to feel the value of their intellectual potential, just as much as we would foster and nurture a really promising young athlete.

We have been considering the contribution that philosophy societies have to make to the cultivation of a school-wide philosophical ethos. A final point to note here is that it is significant that these are identified as 'societies'. A society is an association of individuals which has an identity of its own. Setting things up in this way, as opposed simply to organizing occasional meetings, sends a message to students: here is something you might like to become part of. You don't need to, but if it is 'your thing', then why not sign up? In this way, students are invited to think about whether or not philosophy is something 'for them', and to appreciate the value of joining in with others who share their interest. All of this helps to turn a spark of interest into a steadily burning flame of academic commitment.

What constitutes a society? There needs to be a nucleus of members who can reliably be expected to attend. Out of these, it is good to invite students to take on some of the responsibility for running meetings. For my school Philosophy Society, students make applications for the post of Secretary. Usually, two are appointed. The Secretaries are expected to help advertise meetings, recruit new members, welcome and introduce speakers and sometimes give presentations themselves.

Society meetings are significant events in the term. If there is an opportunity to involve food, this adds to the social dimension of the occasion. It might be something as simple as a soft drink at the end, which provides a chance for students to mingle and keep the discussion going. Or, if time and resources allow, sitting down with students and an invited speaker over a meal greatly adds to the occasion. Eating together is a basic form of human social interaction. It means taking time to be together and relax in each other's company. A meal which is the culmination of an evening of philosophical enquiry often leads to deeper, more personal discussion of the ideas; it is a time when the discussion can be genuine and free of the constraints imposed by a formal classroom or group discussion setting. If time and resources allow, there is nothing like food for encouraging thought.

Appointing a philosopher-in-residence

We have been exploring a model of philosophical education which weaves philosophy throughout the curriculum: one in which philosophical ideas are explored as they emerge within the context of different subjects. I have suggested that a philosophical approach to teaching is one which can be implemented to some extent at least by teachers in most subject areas, and which does not necessarily require extensive specialist knowledge of philosophy.

For schools who want to go further in developing a philosophical ethos, the option of inviting a 'philosopher-in-residence' to join the staff team is one to consider (see Figure 7.2). If a full- or part-time appointment isn't possible, schemes such as the Royal Institute of Philosophy's Jacobsen Trust-Funded 'Philosophy in Schools' programme offer to bring philosophers into schools. There are a number of areas in which a philosopher can work within a school:

- Teaching introductory philosophy as part of a taught course preparation for project work
- Teaching the philosophical elements of religious education
- Teaching citizenship
- Teaching PSHE
- Going into different subjects to explore philosophical ideas through classroom discussion
- Running an extracurricular philosophy club/society
- Assisting with the professional development of staff who are keen to integrate philosophy into their teaching.

Figure 7.2 The philosophical teacher

At Rugby, we were joined by Emma Williams, our Philosopher-in-Residence, in 2008. As well as providing tutorial and teaching support for students working on philosophy projects, part of her role is to go into lessons in other subjects, and explore philosophical ideas with the students in connection with what they are learning. In this way, the work of a philosopher-in-residence embodies one of the main principles being argued for in this book, namely, that philosophy is best done in connection with other subjects. It is worth bearing in mind, when looking to make such appointments, that many philosophy graduates will be able to offer to teach in other subject areas as well. We philosophers are a versatile bunch.

A resident philosopher can also play a role in assisting with the professional development of other staff. Teachers who are keen to explore philosophical and ethical issues within their own discipline can work alongside a resident philosopher, perhaps using a team-teaching approach. In this way, philosophical expertise can be shared. All of this strengthens the philosophical ethos of a school.

The philosophical teacher

The journey into the world of philosophical education is one which promises much: the revitalization of learning; the empowerment of students; a degree of liberation from tedious, restrictive assessment regimes and above all a conception of learning which gives proper place to its intrinsic value – a way of learning in which we discover once again how to enjoy learning for its own sake.

Nowadays, when the goal of education is thought of in terms of acquisition of formal qualifications, and successful education means achieving 'good' results, the rich and significant potential of simply talking with young people about life's deeper questions may seem to have been forgotten. But opportunities for these deeper conversations still exist, if we are prepared to look for them. The Socratic mentor will find that more or less any discussion provides an opportunity for the introduction of philosophical enquiry, with results comparable to those which Socrates encountered: some people are exhilarated, others confused and some infuriated; but all find that they are forced to think again.

To approach your teaching in a Socratic manner is to be constantly looking for ways of stimulating your students to realize that they need to think for themselves, and that it won't do just to lap up what is taught in lessons. In this respect, the Socratic way of doing things is an approach which is diametrically opposed to the style of teaching which an assessment-dominated system tries to pressure us into: teaching-to-the-test; a mechanized, formulaic, didactic regime with little more being asked of students but that they open their mouths as the teacher spoons in easily digestible chunks of information.

Central to all this is the approach of the teacher. If we are going to expect our students to become philosophical learners, those of us who teach have to be philosophical teachers. Following the example of Socrates, this means taking every opportunity to probe, question and challenge the things our students say, until they get the message and begin the process of examining their ideas for themselves.

A philosophical approach to teaching is not one which can be reduced to a set of bullet-pointed lesson plans, and then reproduced with the same arguments, year in, year out. It calls for real thinking and real engagement with questions. Students will quickly detect the difference between a teacher who is themselves genuinely engaged by a problem that is up for discussion and a teacher who is just going through the motions. If you are immersing yourself in a stream of fresh thinking, you will be better placed to invite your students to do the same.

How, in a busy life, with lessons to teach and with all the burdens of educational administration, can a teacher hope to keep alive their own love of learning? Let me offer one concluding suggestion. One way in which some of us have started to meet this need for intellectual refreshment is through a teachers' philosophy reading group. Reading groups are fashionable at the moment – and fun. Teaching is a demanding occupation and teaching in the way in which I am arguing we should is even more demanding, since it means that you cannot approach any two students in the same way. To be effective as a Socratic mentor, you need to be able to engage with the things that the student you are talking to believes and feels. You cannot just begin with a syllabus and a textbook and go from there. Socratic mentoring is inherently personal. So for teachers who are acting in this way, there is even more of a need for a source of intellectual refreshment. Along with colleagues from a range of different disciplines, those of us in the school where I teach who share a love for philosophical discourse have found that a termly (or twice termly, if we are well organized) philosophy reading group meeting, suitably lubricated with some good quality wine, really does help to keep the flame alive. It is a spring to drink from in the midst of the dry land of a long haul through the cycle of teaching, revising and assessing. It is the time when we get to think again.

Epilogue

It is time to think again.

It is time to think again about the end of education.

It is time to think again about our role as teachers.

It is time to think again about Socrates and the rich tradition of philosophy.

It is time to think again about the educational importance of open questions and uncertain answers.

It is time to think again about how best to equip our students with the capacity for critical, reflective enquiry so that they continue their learning journey throughout life.

It is time to think again about the unity of knowledge, so that students learn to think outside curriculum boxes.

It is time to think again about how we assess, and how to have the courage to refuse to allow assessment pressures to constrain us into impoverished teaching.

And if you still think teaching is just about getting your students through those assessment hoops, here is the take-home message: think again!

Bibliography

1994 Group (2008) *New Foundations, Enduring Values.* Available online at www.1994group. ac.uk/documents/public/NewFoundationsEnduringValues.pdf

Augustine (1961) *Confessions.* Translated by Pine-Coffin. Harmondsworth: Penguin.

Baggini, J. (2005) *The Pig That Wants to be Eaten and Ninety-Nine Other Thought Experiments.* London: Grant Books.

— (2009) 'Science and religion don't have to be enemies' in *Herald Scotland.* Available online at www.heraldscotland.com/science-and-religion-don-t-have-to-be-enemies-1.839271

Bentham, J. (1781) *An Introduction to the Principles of Morals and Legislation.* Available online at www.utilitarianism.com/jeremy-bentham/index.html

Blackburn, S. (2010) 'Science, history and philosophy' in P. Derham and M. Worton (eds) *Liberating Learning, Widening Participation.* Buckingham: University of Buckingham Press.

Carey, J. (2005) *What Good are the Arts?* London: Faber and Faber.

Derham, P. and Worton, M. (eds) (2010) *Liberating Learning, Widening Participation.* Buckingham: University of Buckingham Press.

Geach, M. and Gormally, L. (eds) (2005) *Human Life, Ethics and Action.* Exeter: Imprint Academic.

Grayling, A. (2010) 'Liberating learning: Liberal education' in P. Derham and M. Worton (eds) *Liberating Learning, Widening Participation.* Buckingham: University of Buckingham Press.

Hand, M. and Winstanley, C. (eds) *Philosophy in Schools.* London: Continuum.

Hey, S. (2005) 'Seeing both sides of an issue: Teaching an online moral issues course' in *Discourse,* Vol. 5, No. 1, pp. 134–41.

Hume, D. (1910) *An Enquiry Concerning Human Understanding.* Harvard: Collier & Son. Available online at http://18th.eserver.org/hume-enquiry.html

IBO (2011) *The Diploma Programme Curriculum: Core Requirements.* Available online at www.ibo.org/diploma/curriculum/core/essay/

JCQ (2008) *Plagiarism in Examinations.* Available online at www.jcq.org.uk/exams_office/ malpractice/

Levinson, R., Hand, M. and Amos, R. (2008) *A Research Study of the Perspectives on Science AS-Level Course.* University of London: Institute of Education.

Locke, J. (1922) *The Educational Writings of John Locke,* ed. Adamson, J. Cambridge: Cambridge University Press.

McGinn, C. (2006) *Shakespeare's Philosophy.* New York: HarperCollins.

Magee, B. (1987) *The Great Philosophers.* London: BBC Books.

Nussbaum, M. (2010) *Not for Profit: Why Democracy Needs the Humanities*. Princeton: Princeton University Press.

Pope, A. (1870) 'An essay on man' in *Poetical Works*, ed. H. F. Cary. London: Routledge. Available online at http://users.path.ox.ac.uk/~svhunt/PopeVerse.htm

PoS Project Team (2007a) *Perspectives on Science Student Book*. Oxford: Heinemann.

— (2007b) *Perspectives on Science Teacher Resource File*. Oxford: Heinemann.

Pring, R., Hayward, G., Hodgson, A., Johnson, J., Keep, E. and Spours, K. (2009) *Education for All: The Future of Education and Training for 14–19 Year Olds*. London: Routledge.

OCR (2009) *Religious Studies Mark Schemes for the Units A2 H572 AS H172*. Available online at www.ocr.org.uk/download/ms_09/ocr_41072_ms_09_gce_jun.pdf

OFSTED (2010) *Transforming Religious Education: Religious Education in Schools 2006–09*. Available online at www.ofsted.gov.uk/resources/transforming-religious-education

Swinbank, E. and Taylor, J. L. (2009a) *Level 3 Extended Project: Student Guide*. Harlow: Pearson Education.

— (2009b) *Level 3 Extended Project: Teacher Resource Disk*. Harlow: Pearson Education.

UCL (2010) *Auto-Icon*. Available online at www.ucl.ac.uk/Bentham-Project/who/autoicon

Index

Page numbers in **bold** denote figures.